JADEN CROSS

Golang Programming For Beginners

A Step-by-Step Guide to Golang Programming

Contents

Introduction

Why Learn Golang?
In the modern programming landscape, developers have a vast array of languages to choose from, each suited for different tasks. Amid this abundance, Go, also known as Golang, stands out for its unique blend of simplicity, efficiency, and power. Created by Google engineers Robert Griesemer, Rob Pike, and Ken Thompson in 2007, Go was designed to address common frustrations experienced in large-scale software development while maintaining a sense of ease that makes it accessible to newcomers. In this section, we'll explore why learning Go is an excellent decision, whether you're a beginner taking your first steps into programming or an experienced developer looking to enhance your toolkit.

1. Simplicity and Ease of Use

One of the most compelling reasons to learn Go is its simplicity. Go was designed with readability and ease of understanding at its core, making it accessible to beginners without sacrificing power. It follows the philosophy of "less is more," which can be seen in its clean syntax and minimalistic approach to language features.

Go avoids many of the complex features that other languages, such as C++ or Java, implement—like inheritance, templates, and method overloading. Instead, it emphasizes clear and straightforward constructs, which reduces cognitive overhead. This makes Go especially appealing to beginners, as it avoids overwhelming newcomers with complicated concepts.

For example, Go's approach to object-oriented programming (OOP) is simpler than that of traditional OOP languages. It doesn't rely on classes or inheritance, focusing instead on the concept of **interfaces** and **structs**. These structures are easier to grasp and implement, offering an intuitive way to manage data without unnecessary complexity.

Furthermore, Go's syntax encourages good habits right from the start. By mandating certain coding practices, such as consistent formatting and clear error handling, Go helps beginners write clean, maintainable code from the very beginning.

2. Strong Support for Concurrency

In today's computing environment, concurrency is no longer an option; it's a necessity. Whether you're building web applications, data processing systems, or distributed systems, the ability to handle multiple tasks simultaneously is critical to achieving performance at scale. This is where Go truly shines.

Go's concurrency model is simple yet incredibly powerful, allowing developers to write concurrent programs without the usual complexity associated with threads, locks, and semaphores. Go introduces the concept of **goroutines**, lightweight functions that run in the background, which are much cheaper to create and maintain than traditional threads. With goroutines, you can run thousands or even millions of concurrent tasks efficiently.

Alongside goroutines, Go provides **channels**, a mechanism for safe communication between concurrent processes. Channels allow goroutines to synchronize without the need for explicit locking mechanisms, which can lead to complex code and bugs in other languages. This makes Go an excellent choice for writing highly concurrent applications, such as web servers, databases, and cloud-native applications.

For a beginner, learning concurrency in Go is straightforward due to its intuitive design and in-built support. By the time you complete your first Go project, you'll have a solid grasp of concurrency, which is often considered an advanced topic in other programming languages.

3. Performance and Efficiency

While Go is designed to be easy to learn and use, it doesn't compromise on performance. Go is a **compiled language**, meaning the code is translated into machine code that runs directly on the hardware. This is in contrast to interpreted languages like Python or JavaScript, where the code is executed by an intermediary (an interpreter or virtual machine), often resulting in slower performance.

Go's simplicity, combined with its compiled nature, results in high performance with minimal overhead. It has a garbage collector that efficiently manages memory while ensuring that performance-critical applications don't experience the kind of slowdowns typically associated with managed languages like Java or Python.

Additionally, Go's standard library is packed with highly optimized, low-level utilities, which makes it easier for developers to build fast, scalable applications without needing to reach for third-party libraries. The language is particularly well-suited for building networked applications, microservices, and distributed systems—fields where performance is crucial.

4. Go's Versatility Across Domains

Go is a **general-purpose programming language**, meaning it's not confined to any one domain. It is versatile enough to be used in various fields, including web development, systems programming, cloud computing, data science, and more. Whether you're developing backend services, command-line tools, or even AI-powered applications, Go has the tools and frameworks to support your efforts.

Here are some of the key areas where Go excels:

- **Web Development**: With Go's fast execution and easy-to-use HTTP server, it's perfect for building web applications and REST APIs. Popular frameworks like **Gin** and **Echo** simplify the process of setting up web servers.
- **Cloud Computing and Microservices**: Go was designed with modern infrastructure in mind, making it the language of choice for cloud-

native applications and microservices architectures. Tools like **Docker,** **Kubernetes,** and **Terraform,** which power cloud infrastructures, are all written in Go.

- **Systems Programming**: Go offers low-level features like pointers and memory management without the complexities of C or C++. This makes it a great choice for building performance-critical systems applications.
- **DevOps and Tooling**: Go's simplicity and power make it ideal for developing DevOps tools. In fact, many industry-standard tools, including Docker and Kubernetes, are written in Go.

By learning Go, you equip yourself with a language that allows you to work across these various domains, giving you flexibility in your career or personal projects.

5. Excellent Tooling and Ecosystem

A great language is only as good as the ecosystem that surrounds it, and Go excels in this regard. Go's built-in tooling simplifies many tasks that developers encounter in their day-to-day work.

For instance, **gofmt,** a built-in tool, automatically formats your code to adhere to Go's strict style guidelines. This eliminates debates over code style and keeps teams focused on writing clean, maintainable code. Go also comes with built-in support for testing and profiling through the **go test** and **go benchmark** commands, making it easier to write unit tests and measure the performance of your code.

Go's **package manager** and **module system** make dependency management painless. The **go mod** command handles versioning and dependency tracking, ensuring that projects are easily reproducible and maintainable.

Go's ecosystem also includes robust libraries and frameworks for virtually every need. Whether you're working on web development, cloud computing, or system tools, there are high-quality, actively maintained packages available. Popular libraries like **Go-Kit** for microservices, **Gin** for web development, and **gRPC** for API design ensure that Go has what you need, no matter what you're building.

6. Growing Demand and Job Opportunities

Learning Go opens up career opportunities, particularly in the fast-growing fields of cloud computing, distributed systems, and backend development. Go has become the go-to language for large-scale applications that need to handle millions of requests with low latency and high availability. Many leading tech companies, including Google, Uber, Dropbox, and Netflix, use Go to build high-performance services.

Due to its rise in popularity, Go developers are in high demand, and the supply of skilled Go developers is still catching up. This presents an excellent opportunity for those entering the job market or those looking to transition to new roles. Companies are actively seeking developers with Go expertise to help them build the next generation of cloud services, scalable applications, and microservices.

In fact, Go consistently ranks as one of the **highest-paying programming languages** in the tech industry. Its growing adoption by major companies means there's no shortage of job opportunities, from startups to large enterprises. By learning Go, you're positioning yourself as a valuable candidate in the current and future job market.

7. Go's Community and Open Source Contribution

One of the less obvious but equally important reasons to learn Go is its **vibrant and supportive community**. Go has a well-established, enthusiastic developer base, and there are plenty of resources available for learners, from official documentation to tutorials and forums. The community around Go encourages collaboration, and many open-source projects welcome contributions from newcomers.

Additionally, Go has a strong presence in open-source development. Many of the world's most popular open-source projects, like Docker and Kubernetes, are written in Go. This makes Go an attractive language if you're interested in contributing to impactful, widely used software.

Go's community actively works to keep the language stable and backwards compatible, which means that once you learn Go, your skills will remain relevant for a long time. The Go team prioritizes stability and simplicity, ensuring that the language evolves in ways that benefit both beginners and experienced developers.

8. Go's Design Philosophy: Minimalism and Focus

At the heart of Go is a design philosophy that prioritizes simplicity, readability, and maintainability. Unlike other programming languages that evolve by adding more features and increasing complexity, Go takes the opposite approach—it focuses on doing fewer things, but doing them well. This minimalism is evident in Go's syntax and core features, which aim to reduce unnecessary abstractions and encourage developers to write clear, readable code.

This approach makes Go ideal for maintaining large codebases over time. In many organizations, Go is favored for projects where code longevity and maintainability are critical. The simplicity of Go's syntax means that code written years ago is just as easy to read and understand as it was when it was first written.

For beginners, this focus on simplicity is a blessing. You can spend more time learning the language's core concepts without being bogged down by an overwhelming number of features. And for experienced developers, Go's minimalism means you can build and maintain complex systems without having to worry about intricate language nuances.

What is Golang?

Golang, often referred to simply as **Go**, is a statically typed, compiled programming language created at Google. It is designed to be simple, reliable, and efficient, with a focus on ease of use for both novice and experienced programmers. Go's distinguishing features include built-in concurrency support, strong memory safety, and a focus on developer productivity.

Golang was designed to solve real-world problems that developers face when building large-scale, distributed software systems. Its syntax is concise, making code more readable and maintainable, while its rich standard library and powerful tools help streamline development. It is a general-purpose language, suitable for building web servers, cloud applications, command-line tools, and more.

Key Features of Go:

- **Statically Typed**: Go uses static typing, meaning variables must have a type assigned at compile time. This increases performance and minimizes runtime errors.
- **Compiled Language**: Go compiles into machine code, making programs faster than interpreted languages.
- **Concurrency Support**: Go has built-in support for concurrency, allowing you to efficiently manage multiple tasks at once.
- **Garbage Collected**: Go automatically manages memory, freeing developers from manual memory management.
- **Cross-Platform Compatibility**: Go runs on multiple platforms, including Windows, Linux, and macOS, making it highly versatile for modern software development.

History and Evolution of Go

Go was developed in 2007 by three engineers at Google—**Robert Griesemer**, **Rob Pike**, and **Ken Thompson**—who were frustrated by the complexity of managing large-scale software projects using existing languages like C++ and Java. These languages, while powerful, were cumbersome to maintain, and the compilation times were long, slowing down development cycles. The goal was to create a language that would make it easier to build scalable, performant applications with minimal complexity.

Here are some key milestones in Go's evolution:

- **2007**: Development of Go began as an experimental project at Google.
- **2009**: Go was publicly announced and released as an open-source project. It immediately gained attention for its simplicity and promise to solve concurrency and compilation problems.
- **2012**: Go version 1.0 was released, marking the language as stable for production use. This version set the foundation for Go's syntax and

language features that are still present today.

- **2015**: Go 1.5 was released, removing all C dependencies from the language. This was a major step towards making Go a truly independent language for building complex systems.
- **2016-2019**: Go saw rapid adoption in cloud computing, microservices, and web development. Several prominent tools and platforms like Docker and Kubernetes, written in Go, helped boost its popularity.
- **2020s and Beyond**: Go continues to evolve with new features like better dependency management (Go Modules) and planned enhancements in Go 2.0. It remains a highly relevant language for modern development needs, particularly in cloud-native, microservices, and distributed systems.

Why Go Is Perfect for Beginners

Go's design prioritizes simplicity and clarity, making it an ideal language for beginners. Unlike some other languages that can overwhelm newcomers with complex syntax or feature sets, Go provides a clean, straightforward approach to programming.

Here are several reasons why Go is especially suited for beginners:

1. Minimalistic Syntax

Go's syntax is deliberately minimalistic. It avoids complex language features like inheritance, templates, and macros, which can be intimidating for beginners. Instead, Go encourages readable and concise code, allowing learners to focus on understanding core programming concepts like data types, loops, and functions without distractions.

2. Fast Compilation and Execution

For beginners, the fast compile time of Go can make learning more rewarding. Go's compilation process is incredibly quick, meaning that developers can write code, compile, and see results almost instantly. This immediate feedback loop is motivating for learners as they can experiment with their code without long waiting times.

3. Built-in Tools

Go comes with built-in tools like **gofmt** (for formatting code), **go test** (for running unit tests), and **go build** (for compiling applications). These tools are simple to use, help enforce best practices, and are integrated seamlessly into the development workflow. Beginners can focus more on writing code and less on configuring external tools or learning complex build systems.

4. No Unnecessary Complexity

One of Go's biggest strengths is its avoidance of unnecessary complexity. It does not include features like class inheritance or method overloading, which can confuse beginners. Go focuses on doing a few things well, like concurrency, error handling, and structuring programs in a clear, consistent way.

5. Strong Community and Documentation

Go has an extensive community and excellent official documentation. Beginners can easily find resources, tutorials, and forums where they can get help when they encounter challenges. The official Go documentation is also beginner-friendly, providing clear explanations and examples for learning core concepts.

6. Early Exposure to Concurrency

Concurrency is a difficult concept for many programmers to grasp, but Go makes it accessible. With simple constructs like goroutines and channels, beginners can learn to write concurrent programs early on, giving them an edge in understanding modern computing concepts.

Where Go Shines: Concurrency, Web Development, and Microservices

One of Go's most compelling features is its ability to excel in areas where performance, simplicity, and scalability are crucial. These include concurrency, web development, and microservices architecture.

1. Concurrency

Concurrency refers to the ability of a system to perform multiple tasks simultaneously, which is critical in today's multi-core processors and distributed systems. Go's **goroutines** are lightweight threads that allow developers to run functions concurrently without the complexities of traditional multithreading.

- **Goroutines**: Unlike threads, goroutines are incredibly lightweight, and Go can manage thousands of them simultaneously, making it easy to build scalable, efficient programs.
- **Channels**: Go's **channels** allow goroutines to communicate and synchronize without the need for complex lock mechanisms, simplifying the development of concurrent programs.

Because Go's concurrency model is so simple to understand and implement, it's often used for applications that require high performance, such as web servers, real-time systems, and large-scale data processing systems.

2. Web Development

Go's standard library includes everything you need to build robust web applications without relying heavily on third-party frameworks. The **net/http** package provides developers with the ability to create HTTP servers and clients with minimal code. This simplicity, combined with Go's efficiency, makes it a great choice for web development.

- **Lightweight HTTP Servers**: Go's built-in HTTP server is fast, efficient, and can handle a large number of requests concurrently, thanks to Go's concurrency model.
- **Web Frameworks**: Popular frameworks like **Gin** and **Echo** provide additional structure for web development, making it easy to build REST APIs, handle routing, and manage middleware.
- **WebSocket Support**: Go is excellent for real-time applications, such as chat apps or live dashboards, due to its native support for WebSockets and other real-time communication protocols.

3. Microservices

Go has become the go-to language for building **microservices** due to its performance, simplicity, and support for concurrency. In microservices architecture, applications are broken down into smaller, independent services that can be developed, deployed, and scaled independently.

- **Small and Efficient Services**: Go's low memory footprint and fast execution times make it perfect for running multiple small services that interact with each other in a larger system.
- **Cloud-Native and Containerized Applications**: Go works seamlessly with Docker and Kubernetes, the tools that power most cloud-native microservices platforms. In fact, both **Docker** and **Kubernetes** are written in Go, further emphasizing its role in the microservices ecosystem.

Because Go programs compile to a single binary and have minimal dependencies, they are easy to deploy across multiple environments, making Go the perfect choice for cloud-based and containerized applications.

Real-World Use Cases of Go

Go has been adopted by some of the largest tech companies in the world for building highly scalable, performance-critical applications. Let's explore some notable real-world use cases where Go has made a significant impact.

1. Docker

Docker, the popular platform that revolutionized software containerization, was written in Go. Go's fast compile times, concurrency support, and efficiency in managing multiple processes made it the perfect language for Docker. Thanks to Docker, developers can package applications and their dependencies into containers, which can be run consistently across different computing environments.

2. Kubernetes

Kubernetes, the open-source container orchestration system, is also built with Go. It automates the deployment, scaling, and management of containerized applications, and is widely used in cloud computing. Go's concurrency model makes it ideal for handling the distributed nature of Kubernetes.

3. Dropbox

Dropbox, the cloud storage giant, migrated much of its infrastructure from Python to Go to improve performance and scalability. By leveraging Go's concurrency features, Dropbox was able to optimize its systems to handle the vast amounts of data processed by its services.

4. Uber

Uber uses Go to handle high-throughput systems, including geofencing and real-time matching of drivers and riders. Go's ability to handle massive numbers of concurrent requests with low latency has made it invaluable for Uber's infrastructure.

5. Netflix

Netflix has adopted Go for various internal tools, such as building infrastructure services and handling high-concurrency scenarios. Go's simplicity and performance have enabled Netflix to develop robust systems that scale efficiently as the company grows.

Go's real-world applications and powerful features make it a top choice for modern developers. Whether you're interested in building scalable web services, developing microservices for cloud infrastructure, or exploring concurrency in distributed systems, Go offers the right balance of simplicity, power, and performance.

Choosing to learn Golang is a smart investment in your future as a developer. Its simplicity, combined with its power in handling modern-day software challenges like concurrency and cloud computing, makes it an ideal language for beginners and professionals alike. Whether you're building a personal project, working on a startup, or looking to contribute to open-source, Go equips you with the tools and knowledge you need to succeed. With its growing demand in the job market, vast ecosystem, and focus on efficient, maintainable code, Go is a language that will continue to thrive for years to come.

Getting Started with Go

G olang, or Go, has gained widespread popularity due to its simplicity and power. If you're new to Go, this chapter will guide you through the essential steps to get started, including installing the language, setting up a Go workspace, and writing your first Go program. Whether you're working on Windows, macOS, or Linux, you'll be able to hit the ground running with Go by the end of this chapter.

Installing Go on Different Platforms

Before writing your first Go program, you need to install the Go programming language on your machine. Go is cross-platform, meaning it runs on various operating systems like Windows, macOS, and Linux. The installation process is straightforward and takes only a few minutes.

1. Installing Go on Windows

To install Go on a Windows machine, follow these steps:

1. Visit the official Go download page to download the Windows installer.
2. Download the .msi installer for Windows.
3. Run the installer and follow the instructions. The installer automatically sets up the Go environment and adds Go's binaries to the system's PATH.
4. After installation, open a Command Prompt and type the following command to verify the installation:

```
go version
```

1. You should see the Go version number printed, confirming that Go is correctly installed.

2. Installing Go on macOS
If you're using macOS, follow these steps to install Go:

1. Visit the Go download page and download the macOS .pkg installer.
2. Open the downloaded package and follow the installation prompts.
3. After installation, open the Terminal and run:

```
go version
```

1. This will display the installed version of Go.
2. Alternatively, if you prefer using a package manager, you can install Go via **Homebrew** by running:

```
brew install go
```

3. Installing Go on Linux
Installing Go on Linux can be done via a package manager or by downloading the binary release directly. Here's how to do it manually:

1. Download the Linux tarball from the Go download page.
2. Extract the tarball to /usr/local using the following command:

```
sudo tar -C /usr/local -xzf go1.x.x.linux-amd64.tar.gz
```

1. Add Go's binary to your PATH by adding the following line to your .bashrc or .profile:

```
export PATH=$PATH:/usr/local/go/bin
```

1. Apply the changes by running:

```
source ~/.bashrc
```

1. To verify the installation, run:

```
go version
```

Now that you have Go installed on your machine, it's time to set up your development environment.

Setting Up Your First Go Workspace

Once Go is installed, the next step is to set up a **workspace**, which is where all your Go code will reside. A Go workspace is essentially a directory that contains your Go source code, binaries, and dependencies. Go organizes code into **packages**, and each package belongs to a specific module.

1. Understanding Go's Workspace Structure

A typical Go workspace has the following structure:

- **src**: Contains the source code for your projects, organized into packages.
- **pkg**: Contains compiled package objects.
- **bin**: Contains compiled executables.

You don't need to manually create these folders anymore if you're using Go modules (introduced in Go 1.11), as Go modules make workspace management easier and allow you to manage dependencies per project.

2. Setting Up a Go Workspace

To set up your Go workspace:

Create a directory for your workspace. For example:

```
mkdir -p $HOME/go-workspace
```

Inside your workspace, create a src directory where your source code will go:

```
mkdir -p $HOME/go-workspace/src
```

Set your GOPATH to point to your workspace directory by adding the following to your .bashrc or .profile file:

```
export GOPATH=$HOME/go-workspace
export PATH=$PATH:$GOPATH/bin
```

1. This tells Go where to look for your source code, binaries, and dependencies.
2. Apply the changes:

```
source ~/.bashrc
```

1. You can now start creating Go programs inside this workspace.

With Go modules, you don't need to worry about the workspace setup as much, since Go handles dependencies in a project-specific way. Let's now write your first Go program.

Writing Your First Go Program: "Hello, World"

Once you have set up your Go workspace, it's time to write your first Go program. A simple "Hello, World" program is the perfect way to get familiar with Go's syntax and workflow.

In your workspace's src directory, create a new directory for your project:

```
mkdir -p $HOME/go-workspace/src/helloworld
cd helloworld
```

Create a new Go source file named main.go:

```
touch main.go
```

Open main.go in your favorite text editor and add the following code:

```
package main

import "fmt"

func main() {
    fmt.Println("Hello, World!")
}
```

Let's break down this simple program:

- package main: Every Go program must start with a **package declaration**. The main package is special—Go programs start executing from the main function inside this package.
- import "fmt": Go uses **imports** to bring in code from other packages. In this case, we are importing the fmt package, which contains functions for formatting text, including printing to the console.
- func main() {}: The **main function** is the entry point for Go programs. When you run your program, Go will execute this function.
- fmt.Println("Hello, World!"): This line calls the Println function from the fmt package to print "Hello, World!" to the console.

1. To run the program, use the Go command:

```
go run main.go
```

1. You should see the following output:

```
Hello, World!
```

Congratulations, you've written and executed your first Go program! Let's now explore how Go organizes source code and manages dependencies.

Understanding Go's File Structure and Workflows

Go organizes source code into **packages**, and every Go program consists of multiple packages. Understanding how packages work is essential for creating modular and reusable code.

1. Packages in Go

In Go, a package is simply a collection of related Go source files that are organized together under a common namespace. Every Go source file must declare which package it belongs to at the top of the file.

Here are the two main types of packages in Go:

- **Executable Packages**: These are packages that include a main function and can be run as a standalone program. The main package we used in the "Hello, World" example is an executable package.
- **Library Packages**: These are packages meant to be imported and used by other packages. They don't contain a main function and are used to share reusable code.

2. The Go Build Process

Go follows a straightforward build process. When you run a Go program, Go performs the following steps:

1. **Compiles the source code** into machine code.
2. **Links any external packages** that are imported by the program.
3. **Generates an executable binary** that you can run on your machine.

You can use the following Go commands to manage your projects:

- **go build**: Compiles your code and produces an executable binary.
- **go run**: Compiles and runs your Go program without producing a binary.
- **go install**: Compiles and installs the binary into the $GOPATH/bin directory.

Let's compile your "Hello, World" program using the go build command:

```
go build
```

This command creates an executable file named helloworld (or helloworld.exe on Windows). You can then run this binary directly:

```
./helloworld
```

3. Go Modules: Dependency Management Made Easy

In Go, **modules** are used to manage dependencies. A Go module is a collection of Go packages, and it defines how those packages are versioned and distributed.

To create a new module for your project:

1. Inside your project directory, initialize a new module:

```
go mod init helloworld
```

1. This creates a go.mod file that tracks your project's dependencies.
2. If your project imports external packages, Go automatically updates the go.mod file to include those dependencies and their versions.

For example, if you add an external package like "github.com/go-sql-driver/mysql" to your imports, Go will automatically handle downloading and managing the package for you. This simplifies dependency management, especially for larger projects.

Next Steps: Moving Beyond "Hello, World"

Now that you've successfully set up Go and written your first program, you're ready to move on to more advanced topics. You've learned how to install Go, set up a workspace, write and run Go code, and manage dependencies with Go modules. In the next chapter, we'll dive deeper into Go's syntax, including variables, data types, and functions, giving you the tools to write more complex and functional programs.

By the end of this book, you'll have mastered the fundamentals of Go and be ready to build scalable, concurrent applications that can handle real-world tasks.

Go Basics – Variables, Data Types, and Functions

I n this chapter, we will explore the core building blocks of programming in Go: variables, data types, and functions. Understanding these concepts is fundamental to writing effective Go programs. By mastering how to declare and use variables, work with different data types, and write functions, you'll gain the skills necessary to start building more complex applications.

Declaring Variables in Go

Variables in Go are used to store and manage data throughout your program. Unlike some other languages, Go requires that every variable has a type, and it is strictly enforced by the compiler. This helps avoid many errors and ensures that programs behave predictably.

Go provides several ways to declare variables, and it's important to understand the syntax options.

1. Using the var Keyword

The simplest way to declare a variable in Go is by using the var keyword. This approach allows you to specify the variable's type explicitly.

```
var name string
name = "Alice"
```

Here, we declare a variable name of type string. We can then assign the value

21

"Alice" to this variable.

Alternatively, you can declare and initialize the variable in one step:

```
var age int = 30
```

This declares an integer variable age and assigns it a value of 30. Go is strongly typed, so once a variable's type is defined, you cannot assign a value of a different type to that variable.

2. Short Variable Declaration (:=)

Go allows you to declare and initialize variables more concisely using the := operator. This is a shorthand syntax that infers the type based on the value you assign to the variable.

```
name := "Alice"
age  := 30
```

In this case, Go automatically determines that name is a string and age is an int. This shorthand declaration can only be used inside functions, making it a useful tool for local variable declarations.

3. Multiple Variable Declarations

Go allows you to declare multiple variables at once, which can simplify your code when dealing with several variables of different types.

```
var x, y, z int = 1, 2, 3
```

In this example, x, y, and z are all declared as integers and initialized with values 1, 2, and 3, respectively.

You can also mix types when declaring multiple variables:

```
var name, age, isStudent = "Alice", 30, true
```

Here, Go automatically infers that name is a string, age is an int, and isStudent is a bool.

4. Zero Values

In Go, variables are always initialized with a **zero value** if not explicitly initialized. For example, an int variable will have a default value of 0, and a string will have a default value of "" (empty string). Understanding this behavior can help avoid bugs in your code when working with uninitialized variables.

```
var count int   // count is initialized to 0
var message string  // message is initialized to an empty string
```

Built-in Data Types: int, string, float, bool

Go provides several built-in data types, each designed to handle specific types of data. Let's explore the most commonly used ones.

1. Integer Types

Go has several integer types, including int, int8, int16, int32, and int64, which represent signed integers of varying sizes. The int type is most commonly used and represents a signed integer whose size depends on the platform (32-bit or 64-bit).

```
var age int = 30
```

Go also supports unsigned integer types like uint, uint8, uint16, uint32, and uint64, which represent non-negative integers.

```
var distance uint = 100
```

2. Floating Point Types

Go provides floating-point types for handling decimal numbers: float32 and float64. By default, Go uses float64 for floating-point numbers due to its higher precision.

```
var price float64 = 9.99
```

If precision is not critical, you can use float32 for smaller floating-point values:

```
var smallNumber float32 = 3.14
```

3. String Type

Strings in Go represent a sequence of characters. They are immutable, meaning once a string is created, it cannot be modified. Go uses double quotes to define string literals.

```
var greeting string = "Hello, World!"
```

Strings can also be concatenated using the + operator:

```
message := "Hello, " + "Alice"
```

4. Boolean Type

The boolean data type, bool, represents true/false values. It is typically used in control flow statements like if or for.

```
var isLoggedIn bool = true
```

You can declare and initialize boolean variables using logical expressions:

```
isValid := (5 > 3)  // true
```

5. Constants

In addition to variables, Go allows you to define constants using the const keyword. Constants are values that cannot be changed once they are defined.

```
const pi = 3.14
```

Constants can be of any basic data type (int, float, string, etc.), and they are useful for values that remain unchanged throughout the program.

Introduction to Functions

Functions in Go are the building blocks of any Go program. They allow you to encapsulate reusable blocks of code, making your programs more modular and maintainable.

1. Defining Functions

A function in Go is defined using the func keyword, followed by the function's name, parameters, return type (if any), and the function body.

Here's a basic function that adds two numbers:

```
func add(x int, y int) int {
    return x + y
}
```

Let's break this down:

- **func**: The keyword that starts a function declaration.
- **add**: The name of the function.
- **x int, y int**: The function parameters. This function accepts two integer arguments, x and y.
- **int**: The return type of the function. This function returns an integer.
- **return x + y**: The function body. The return statement sends the result of the addition back to the caller.

You can call this function like so:

```
sum := add(3, 4)   // sum now holds the value 7
```

2. Functions with Multiple Return Values

Go supports functions that return multiple values, a feature that simplifies error handling and improves code readability.

For example, a function that divides two numbers and returns both the result and a potential error can be written like this:

```go
func divide(x, y float64) (float64, error) {
    if y == 0 {
        return 0, fmt.Errorf("division by zero")
    }
    return x / y, nil
}
```

Here, the function returns both a float64 (the result) and an error (which is nil if no error occurs).

You can handle multiple return values like this:

```go
result, err := divide(10, 2)
if err != nil {
    fmt.Println("Error:", err)
} else {
    fmt.Println("Result:", result)
}
```

3. Named Return Values

Go allows you to name the return values in a function definition. This can improve code clarity, particularly in more complex functions.

```go
func rectangleArea(width, height float64) (area float64) {
    area = width * height
    return
}
```

In this example, the return value area is named, and Go automatically returns it when the function reaches the end.

4. Variadic Functions

Go supports **variadic functions**, which are functions that can accept a variable number of arguments. Variadic functions use the ... syntax to indicate that they can take an arbitrary number of arguments of a given type.

Here's an example of a variadic function that sums a list of integers:

```go
func sum(numbers ...int) int {
    total := 0
    for _, number := range numbers {
        total += number
    }
    return total
}
```

You can call this function with any number of arguments:

```go
result := sum(1, 2, 3, 4, 5)  // result = 15
```

Variadic functions are useful when you want to pass an unknown number of arguments to a function, such as in a logging function that takes a variable number of messages.

Scope and Lifetime of Variables

Variables in Go have a scope, which defines where in the program they can be accessed. Understanding variable scope is crucial for writing clear and error-free programs.

1. Local Variables

Variables declared inside a function are local to that function and cannot be accessed outside of it. These variables are created when the function is called and destroyed when the function exits.

```go
func greet() {
    name := "Alice"  // local variable
    fmt.Println("Hello,", name)
}
```

Here, the variable name is local to the greet function and cannot be accessed outside of it.

2. Global Variables

Global variables are declared outside of any function and can be accessed by any part of the program. Global variables can be useful for storing values that need to be shared across multiple functions.

```go
var counter int = 0  // global variable

func increment() {
    counter++
}
```

In this example, counter is a global variable that can be accessed and modified by both the increment function and any other part of the program.

3. Block-Level Scope

Variables declared within a block (such as an if, for, or switch block) are only accessible within that block.

```go
func checkNumber(num int) {
    if num > 0 {
        result := "positive"  // block-scoped variable
        fmt.Println(result)
    }
}
```

The variable result is only accessible inside the if block and cannot be used outside of it.

In this chapter, we explored the foundational concepts of Go programming, including variables, data types, and functions. We learned how to declare variables, work with different data types, and write functions to encapsulate reusable code. By mastering these basics, you now have the essential tools to begin writing more complex and efficient Go programs.

As you continue your journey with Go, remember that practice is key. Experiment with different data types, create functions that perform meaningful tasks, and explore how Go's type system helps prevent errors. In the next chapter, we'll delve into control structures and error handling, which will further enhance your ability to write robust Go applications.

Control Structures and Error Handling

Control structures and error handling are essential aspects of any programming language, and Go is no exception. They allow you to manage the flow of your program, make decisions, and handle unforeseen issues gracefully. In this chapter, we will explore Go's control structures, including conditionals and loops, as well as Go's approach to error handling, which is unique compared to other languages.

Conditional Statements: if, else, switch

Control structures enable your programs to make decisions based on the data they receive or generate. Go provides powerful yet simple mechanisms for writing conditionals through the if, else, and switch statements.

1. The if Statement

The if statement is one of the simplest ways to introduce logic into your programs. It evaluates a boolean expression, and if the expression evaluates to true, the code inside the block is executed.

Here's a basic example of an if statement:

```
x := 10

if x > 5 {
    fmt.Println("x is greater than 5")
}
```

In this example, since x is greater than 5, the program prints "x is greater than 5."

2. The else Statement

Often, you'll want to specify an alternative action if the if condition is not met. This is done using the else statement.

```
x := 3

if x > 5 {
    fmt.Println("x is greater than 5")
} else {
    fmt.Println("x is less than or equal to 5")
}
```

Since x is less than or equal to 5 in this case, the else block is executed.

3. The else if Statement

When you have multiple conditions to check, you can use the else if statement. It allows you to evaluate several conditions in sequence.

```
x := 5

if x > 10 {
    fmt.Println("x is greater than 10")
} else if x == 5 {
    fmt.Println("x is equal to 5")
} else {
    fmt.Println("x is less than 5")
}
```

In this example, the program checks three conditions, and since x is equal to 5, the second condition is met, and "x is equal to 5" is printed.

4. Declaring Variables in if Statements

Go allows you to declare variables directly inside an if statement, which can be useful when you only need a variable within the scope of that condition. This feature helps to reif result := calculateSomething(); result > 10 {

31

```
fmt.Println("Result is greater than 10")
}
```

In this example, the variable result is declared and initialized inside the if statement. It is only accessible within the scope of the if block.

5. The switch Statement

In Go, the switch statement offers an elegant way to handle multiple conditions. It's often used as a cleaner alternative to a series of if-else statements.

Here's a basic switch statement:

```
day := "Monday"

switch day {
case "Monday":
    fmt.Println("Start of the workweek")
case "Friday":
    fmt.Println("End of the workweek")
default:
    fmt.Println("Midweek")
}
```

In this example, the program checks the value of day and prints the corresponding message. If no cases match, the default case is executed.

One of the advantages of Go's switch statement is that you don't need to include explicit break statements as in other languages. Each case is automatically terminated after execution, preventing fall-through by default.

6. Expression-less switch Statements

Go allows you to omit the expression in the switch statement, turning it into a powerful alternative to multiple if-else blocks.

```
x := 10

switch {
case x > 5:
```

```
    fmt.Println("x is greater than 5")
case x < 5:
    fmt.Println("x is less than 5")
default:
    fmt.Println("x is equal to 5")
}
```

In this version of switch, the first true condition is executed. This approach is handy when dealing with multiple ranges or conditions.

Loops in Go: The for Loop

Loops allow you to repeat blocks of code based on certain conditions. In Go, the for loop is the only looping construct, but it is highly flexible and can be used in a variety of ways.

1. Basic for Loop

The most common form of a for loop in Go is similar to the loops found in languages like C and Java.

```
for i := 0; i < 10; i++ {
    fmt.Println(i)
}
```

This loop starts with i = 0, runs until i is less than 10, and increments i after each iteration. It prints the numbers 0 through 9.

2. for as a While Loop

Go doesn't have a while loop, but the for loop can be used to achieve the same functionality. A for loop without initialization or post statements behaves like a traditional while loop.

```
x := 0
for x < 5 {
    fmt.Println(x)
    x++
}
```

This loop continues running as long as the condition x < 5 is true.

3. Infinite Loop

You can create an infinite loop in Go using the for loop by omitting all conditions.

```
for {
    fmt.Println("Running indefinitely")
}
```

This loop will run forever unless you explicitly break out of it using the break statement.

4. Breaking and Continuing Loops

To exit a loop prematurely, you can use the break statement. To skip the current iteration and move to the next, you can use the continue statement.

```
for i := 0; i < 10; i++ {
    if i == 5 {
        break   // exit the loop when i equals 5
    }
    fmt.Println(i)
}
```

```
for i := 0; i < 10; i++ {
    if i%2 == 0 {
        continue   // skip even numbers
    }
    fmt.Println(i)
}
```

In the first example, the loop exits when i equals 5. In the second example, the continue statement skips the even numbers, printing only the odd ones.

5. Range-Based for Loops

The for loop can also be used to iterate over collections such as arrays, slices, maps, and strings using the range keyword.

```
names := []string{"Alice", "Bob", "Charlie"}

for index, name := range names {
    fmt.Printf("Index: %d, Name: %s\n", index, name)
}
```

In this example, the loop iterates over the slice names, and the range keyword returns both the index and the value for each iteration. You can omit the index or value if they are not needed by using an underscore (_).

Error Handling in Go: A Unique Approach

Go's approach to error handling is different from many other languages. Instead of using exceptions, Go handles errors explicitly through return values. This encourages developers to write robust, error-aware code and makes error handling a first-class part of the programming experience.

1. Returning Errors from Functions

In Go, errors are handled by returning an error type from a function. The built-in error type is used to represent errors, and functions that can fail usually return an additional error value alongside their result.

```
func divide(x, y float64) (float64, error) {
    if y == 0 {
        return 0, fmt.Errorf("cannot divide by zero")
    }
    return x / y, nil
}
```

In this example, the divide function returns a float64 result and an error. If y is 0, an error is returned; otherwise, the division result is returned.

To handle the error, you can check the returned error value:

```
result, err := divide(10, 0)
if err != nil {
    fmt.Println("Error:", err)
} else {
    fmt.Println("Result:", result)
}
```

In this case, the program prints the error message, "cannot divide by zero."

2. Creating Custom Errors

Go allows you to create your own error messages using the fmt.Errorf function. This is useful when you need more specific or informative error messages.

```
func sqrt(x float64) (float64, error) {
    if x < 0 {
        return 0, fmt.Errorf("cannot compute the square root of a
        negative number: %f", x)
    }
    return math.Sqrt(x), nil
}
```

Here, the sqrt function returns a custom error message if a negative number is passed to it.

3. Using the errors Package

Go's standard library provides the errors package, which contains useful functions for working with errors. For example, you can create an error using errors.New:

```
import "errors"

var errNegativeNumber = errors.New("cannot compute the square
root of a negative number")

func sqrt(x float64) (float64, error) {
    if x < 0 {
```

```
        return 0, errNegativeNumber
    }
    return math.Sqrt(x), nil
}
```

In this example, errNegativeNumber is a predefined error, which you can return when an invalid input is encountered.

4. Panic and Recover

In addition to Go's standard error handling mechanism, Go also provides the panic and recover functions for handling unexpected or critical errors.

- **Panic:** The panic function stops the normal flow of execution and unwinds the stack, causing the program to crash unless recover is used.
- **Recover:** The recover function allows you to regain control after a panic, making it possible to handle critical errors gracefully.

```
func main() {
    defer func() {
        if r := recover(); r != nil {
            fmt.Println("Recovered from:", r)
        }
    }()
    panic("Something went wrong")
}
```

In this example, the program panics, but the deferred function with recover catches the panic, allowing the program to continue without crashing completely.

Best Practices for Error Handling

Go encourages a proactive approach to error handling. Here are some best practices to keep in mind:

- **Check errors immediately**: Always check for errors right after a function returns, and handle them accordingly.
- **Return early**: If an error occurs, return from the function early. This keeps your code cleaner and more readable.
- **Wrap errors for context**: When propagating errors up the call stack, add context to the error to make it easier to debug.

```
result, err := divide(10, 0)
if err != nil {
    fmt.Printf("Failed to divide: %v\n", err)
    return
}
```

In this chapter, we've explored Go's control structures and its unique approach to error handling. You now have the tools to manage the flow of your programs using if, else, switch, and for loops, and you've learned how to handle errors explicitly by returning them from functions.

Mastering control structures and error handling is essential for writing robust Go applications. As you practice these concepts, you'll find that Go's design encourages clean, error-aware code, which will help you build more reliable and maintainable software.

In the next chapter, we'll dive deeper into working with arrays, slices, and maps—Go's essential data structures for storing and manipulating collections of data.

Working with Arrays, Slices, and Maps

G o provides several powerful built-in data structures that allow developers to store and manipulate collections of data. **Arrays, slices**, and **maps** are foundational tools in Go that help manage lists of items, dynamic collections, and key-value pairs. In this chapter, we will explore each of these data structures in detail, understanding their characteristics and use cases, along with practical examples that illustrate how to utilize them effectively.

Arrays in Go: Fixed-Length Sequences

Arrays in Go are a collection of elements of the same type, stored in a contiguous block of memory. They have a fixed length, which means the size of the array cannot be changed once it is declared. Although arrays are fundamental in Go, their fixed size often makes them less flexible compared to slices (which we will discuss later).

1. Declaring and Initializing Arrays

You can declare an array in Go by specifying the length of the array and the type of its elements. Here's how you declare an array of integers with a length of 5:

```
var numbers [5]int
```

This creates an array called numbers that can store five integers, all initialized to the zero value of int, which is 0.

Alternatively, you can initialize the array with values during declaration:

```
numbers := [5]int{10, 20, 30, 40, 50}
```

Here, the array numbers is initialized with the values 10, 20, 30, 40, and 50.

2. Accessing and Modifying Array Elements

Array elements are accessed using zero-based indexing. You can retrieve or modify individual elements by referring to their index:

```
fmt.Println(numbers[0])    // Output: 10
numbers[1] = 25            // Change the second element to 25
fmt.Println(numbers[1])    // Output: 25
```

In this example, we accessed the first element using numbers[0], and we modified the second element by assigning a new value to numbers[1].

3. Iterating Over Arrays

You can use a for loop to iterate over arrays. The range keyword is particularly useful for looping through all the elements in an array.

```
for index, value := range numbers {
    fmt.Printf("Index: %d, Value: %d\n", index, value)
}
```

This loop will print each index and the corresponding value in the numbers array.

4. Multi-Dimensional Arrays

Go also supports multi-dimensional arrays, which are arrays of arrays. For example, you can declare a 2D array (an array of arrays) like this:

```
var matrix [3][3]int
```

This creates a 3x3 matrix of integers, where each element is initialized to 0. You can access or modify elements using two indices:

```
matrix[0][0] = 1
matrix[1][2] = 5
fmt.Println(matrix)
```

Multi-dimensional arrays are useful in situations where you need to represent grids or matrices, such as in games or mathematical applications.

5. Limitations of Arrays

While arrays can be useful, their fixed size often makes them less practical for many real-world applications where dynamic resizing is needed. This is where slices come in as a more flexible alternative.

Slices: Go's Dynamic Array Type

A **slice** is a more flexible, powerful data structure in Go that builds on top of arrays. Unlike arrays, slices are dynamic—meaning they can grow or shrink in size during runtime. Slices are widely used in Go due to their versatility and efficiency, as they provide all the benefits of arrays without the limitations of fixed size.

1. Declaring and Initializing Slices

Slices can be declared similarly to arrays, but without specifying the length. You can create a slice using the [] syntax:

```
var numbers []int  // A slice of integers
```

Slices are often initialized with a literal of values:

```
numbers := []int{10, 20, 30, 40, 50}
```

You can also use the make function to create slices with a specific length and capacity:

```
numbers := make([]int, 5)  // A slice with length 5 and capacity 5
```

The first argument to make specifies the type ([]int), while the second

41

argument specifies the slice's length (5 in this case).

2. Accessing and Modifying Slice Elements

You can access and modify slice elements in the same way as arrays, using zero-based indexing:

```
fmt.Println(numbers[0])   // Access the first element
numbers[2] = 35           // Modify the third element
```

Slices have the added advantage that their size can grow or shrink as needed.

3. Slicing a Slice

One of the most powerful features of Go's slices is the ability to take a **slice of a slice**. You can create a new slice by extracting a subrange of elements from an existing slice:

```
subslice := numbers[1:4]  // Extract elements from index 1 to 3
fmt.Println(subslice)     // Output: [20, 30, 40]
```

This new slice, subslice, is a view of the original numbers slice, sharing the same underlying array.

4. Slice Capacity and Length

Slices have two important properties: **length** and **capacity**. The length is the number of elements in the slice, while the capacity is the number of elements in the underlying array, starting from the first element in the slice.

```
fmt.Println(len(numbers))  // Length of the slice
fmt.Println(cap(numbers))  // Capacity of the slice
```

Length can change as you append or remove elements from the slice, but capacity is fixed based on the underlying array. When the slice exceeds its capacity, Go automatically allocates a new, larger array and copies the existing elements.

5. Appending to a Slice

Go's built-in append function makes it easy to add elements to a slice. The append function returns a new slice with the added element(s).

```
numbers = append(numbers, 60)
fmt.Println(numbers)  // Output: [10, 20, 30, 40, 50, 60]
```

If the slice's capacity is exceeded, Go allocates more memory and resizes the slice behind the scenes.

You can also append multiple elements at once:

```
numbers = append(numbers, 70, 80, 90)
fmt.Println(numbers)  // Output: [10, 20, 30, 40, 50, 60, 70, 80,
90]
```

6. Copying Slices

Go provides the copy function, which allows you to copy elements from one slice to another. The number of elements copied is the smaller of the length of the two slices.

```
source := []int{1, 2, 3}
destination := make([]int, len(source))
copy(destination, source)
fmt.Println(destination)  // Output: [1, 2, 3]
```

This copies all elements from source to destination.

7. Slice Internals and Memory Sharing

One key detail about slices is that they share the same underlying array with other slices derived from them. This means that modifying one slice may affect other slices that refer to the same data.

For example:

```
a := []int{1, 2, 3, 4, 5}
b := a[1:4]
b[0] = 10
fmt.Println(a)  // Output: [1, 10, 3, 4, 5]
```

```
fmt.Println(b)  // Output: [10, 3, 4]
```

In this case, modifying b also changes a because they share the same underlying array. Be mindful of this when working with slices in real-world applications.

Maps: Key-Value Pairs in Go

Maps in Go are unordered collections of key-value pairs, where each key is unique, and each key maps to a corresponding value. Maps are highly efficient for lookups and are widely used when you need to associate values with specific keys.

1. Declaring and Initializing Maps

Maps are declared using the map keyword, followed by the types of the key and the value:

```
var scores map[string]int
```

In this case, scores is a map where the keys are strings (e.g., names), and the values are integers (e.g., scores). You can initialize a map using the make function:

```
scores = make(map[string]int)
```

Alternatively, you can declare and initialize a map with values in one step:

```
scores := map[string]int{
    "Alice": 95,
    "Bob":   80,
}
```

2. Adding, Accessing, and Modifying Map Elements

You can add new key-value pairs to a map or update existing ones using the assignment operator:

```
scores["Charlie"] = 85
```

To access a value in a map, use the key:

```
fmt.Println(scores["Alice"])   // Output: 95
```

You can modify an existing value by assigning a new value to the key:

```
scores["Bob"] = 90
```

3. Checking if a Key Exists

Go provides a simple way to check if a key exists in a map. You can use the value, ok idiom to determine whether the key is present:

```
score, ok := scores["Dave"]
if ok {
    fmt.Println("Score:", score)
} else {
    fmt.Println("Dave not found")
}
```

In this case, ok will be false if the key "Dave" is not found in the map.

4. Deleting Elements from a Map

You can remove a key-value pair from a map using the delete function:

```
delete(scores, "Alice")
fmt.Println(scores)  // "Alice" is removed from the map
```

5. Iterating Over Maps

You can use a for loop with the range keyword to iterate over the keys and values of a map:

```go
for name, score := range scores {
    fmt.Printf("Name: %s, Score: %d\n", name, score)
}
```

This loop prints each key-value pair in the scores map.

6. Maps as Function Arguments

Maps in Go are reference types, meaning that when you pass a map to a function, the function receives a reference to the original map. Any changes made to the map inside the function will affect the original map.

Here's an example:

```go
func addScore(scores map[string]int, name string, score int) {
    scores[name] = score
}

scores := make(map[string]int)
addScore(scores, "Alice", 95)
fmt.Println(scores)  // Output: map[Alice:95]
```

Changes to scores inside the addScore function are reflected in the original scores map.

In this chapter, we explored Go's essential data structures: arrays, slices, and maps. Arrays offer fixed-length, contiguous blocks of memory, while slices provide a flexible, resizable view over arrays. Maps, on the other hand, enable you to store and retrieve values using unique keys, making them highly efficient for tasks involving lookups and associations.

By understanding and mastering these data structures, you now have powerful tools at your disposal to handle collections of data effectively in Go. In the next chapter, we'll dive into **structs, methods, and interfaces**, which will allow you to define custom types and organize your code in a more modular and reusable way.

Structs, Methods, and Interfaces

I n Go, **structs**, **methods**, and **interfaces** provide a flexible and powerful way to structure your programs and represent data. These concepts allow you to group related data together, define functions that operate on that data, and create abstractions that make your code modular and reusable. Structs, methods, and interfaces form the backbone of Go's approach to object-oriented programming, without the complexity found in traditional OOP languages.

In this chapter, we'll explore each of these concepts in depth, including practical examples of how to use them in real-world scenarios.

Structs: Custom Data Types

In Go, a **struct** is a composite data type that allows you to group together variables, known as fields, under a single type. Structs are the primary way to represent and organize data in Go, and they enable you to model real-world entities with various attributes.

1. Declaring and Initializing Structs

To define a struct, you use the type keyword followed by the name of the struct and the struct fields.

```
type Person struct {
    Name string
    Age  int
}
```

In this example, we define a Person struct with two fields: Name (of type string) and Age (of type int). Once you've defined the struct, you can create instances of it.

```
var alice Person
alice.Name = "Alice"
alice.Age = 30
```

Alternatively, you can initialize a struct with values at the time of creation:

```
bob := Person{Name: "Bob", Age: 25}
```

If you leave out some fields, Go will initialize them to their zero values:

```
charlie := Person{Name: "Charlie"}  // Age is initialized to 0
```

2. Accessing and Modifying Struct Fields

You can access and modify struct fields using dot notation:

```
fmt.Println(bob.Name)   // Output: Bob
bob.Age = 26            // Change Bob's age
fmt.Println(bob.Age)    // Output: 26
```

Structs allow you to group related data, making your programs easier to manage and understand.

3. Struct Literals

You can also create a struct instance using a **struct literal**, which allows you to initialize a struct without specifying the field names. However, this requires you to initialize fields in the order they are defined in the struct type:

```
dave := Person{"Dave", 40} // Struct literal with positional
arguments
```

This approach is concise but less readable when working with structs that have many fields, as the meaning of each value is not immediately obvious.

4. Pointers to Structs

Structs in Go can be passed by value or by reference using pointers. When passing a struct by value, Go creates a copy of the struct. If you want to modify the original struct, you should pass a pointer to the struct instead.

Here's how to create a pointer to a struct:

```
p := &Person{Name: "Eve", Age: 35}
```

You can then access the fields of the struct through the pointer without having to dereference it explicitly:

```
fmt.Println(p.Name)    // Go automatically dereferences the pointer
p.Age = 36             // Modify the original struct through the
pointer
fmt.Println(p.Age)     // Output: 36
```

Go automatically handles dereferencing pointers to structs, making the syntax more concise.

Methods: Functions with Struct Receivers

In Go, a **method** is simply a function that is associated with a specific type, usually a struct. Methods allow you to define behavior for your structs, enabling you to operate on struct data using clean, intuitive syntax.

1. Defining Methods

To define a method for a struct, you use the func keyword, followed by the method name, a **receiver** argument (the struct it operates on), and the method body.

```
func (p Person) Greet() {
    fmt.Printf("Hello, my name is %s and I am %d years old.\n",
    p.Name, p.Age)
}
```

Here, Greet is a method associated with the Person struct. The receiver, (p Person), specifies that the method operates on a Person instance. You can call the method on any instance of Person:

```
bob.Greet()  // Output: Hello, my name is Bob and I am 25 years
old.
```

2. Pointer vs Value Receivers

Go allows you to define methods with either **value receivers** or **pointer receivers**. A value receiver operates on a copy of the struct, while a pointer receiver operates on the original struct, allowing the method to modify the struct's fields.

Here's an example of a method with a pointer receiver:

```
func (p *Person) HaveBirthday() {
    p.Age += 1
}
```

This method modifies the Age field of the Person struct. Since it uses a pointer receiver, it can change the original struct:

```
bob.HaveBirthday()
fmt.Println(bob.Age)  // Output: 26
```

You should use pointer receivers when you need to modify the struct or when copying the struct would be inefficient (e.g., for large structs).

3. Methods vs Functions

While methods are tied to specific types, functions are not. A method can access and modify the fields of the struct it is attached to, while a function cannot. Methods help you define behaviors that are closely related to the data they operate on.

Interfaces: Abstractions in Go

Interfaces in Go define a set of method signatures but do not provide implementations. They allow you to define abstract types that can be implemented by different structs, enabling polymorphism and flexible program design.

1. Defining Interfaces

An interface in Go is defined using the type keyword, followed by a set of method signatures. For example, here's a Speaker interface that requires the implementation of the Speak method:

```
type Speaker interface {
    Speak()
}
```

Any type that provides a method matching the Speak signature implicitly implements the Speaker interface. In Go, there is no need to explicitly declare that a type implements an interface.

2. Implementing Interfaces

Let's implement the Speaker interface for the Person struct by defining a Speak method:

```
func (p Person) Speak() {
    fmt.Printf("Hello, my name is %s.\n", p.Name)
}
```

Now, any Person can be treated as a Speaker:

```
var s Speaker = bob
s.Speak()  // Output: Hello, my name is Bob.
```

The power of interfaces lies in their ability to allow multiple types to implement the same behavior. For example, you can create another struct, Dog, that also implements the Speaker interface:

```
type Dog struct {
    Name string
}

func (d Dog) Speak() {
    fmt.Printf("Woof! My name is %s.\n", d.Name)
}

dog := Dog{Name: "Buddy"}
s = dog
s.Speak()  // Output: Woof! My name is Buddy.
```

Now both Person and Dog implement the Speaker interface, and Go can treat both types polymorphically as Speaker.

3. Interface Composition

Go supports **interface composition**, where an interface can include other interfaces. For example:

```
type Walker interface {
    Walk()
}

type Speaker interface {
    Speak()
}

type Person interface {
    Speaker
    Walker
}
```

In this case, any type that implements both Speak and Walk automatically satisfies the Person interface.

4. Empty Interface and Type Assertions

The **empty interface** (interface{}) is a special interface that any type satisfies, making it a powerful tool for generic programming. Since all types implement the empty interface, it can hold values of any type:

```
var anything interface{}
anything = 42
fmt.Println(anything)   // Output: 42
anything = "Hello"
fmt.Println(anything)   // Output: Hello
```

To retrieve the actual value stored in an interface{}, you need to perform a **type assertion**:

```
if value, ok := anything.(int); ok {
    fmt.Println("The value is an int:", value)
} else {
    fmt.Println("The value is not an int")
}
```

In this example, we check if anything holds an int. If the assertion is successful, we can access the value as an int; otherwise, we handle the case where the value is not of the expected type.

5. Practical Use of Interfaces

Interfaces are a powerful tool in Go, especially when you want to write flexible and modular code. For instance, if you are writing a logging system, you can define an interface Logger with methods like LogInfo and LogError, and implement it for different types of logging (e.g., to a file, to the console, etc.).

```
type Logger interface {
    LogInfo(message string)
    LogError(err error)
}
```

Each implementation can handle logging in its own way, but any function that accepts a Logger interface can work with any logging system.

Embedding in Go: Structs and Interfaces

Embedding is a powerful feature in Go that allows you to embed one struct or interface inside another. This is Go's way of achieving a form of inheritance while maintaining simplicity and clarity.

1. Struct Embedding

Struct embedding allows one struct to be used as a field within another struct, giving the outer struct access to the inner struct's fields and methods.

```
type Employee struct {
    Person
    Position string
    Salary   int
}
```

In this example, Employee embeds the Person struct, meaning that Employee now has access to all of Person's fields and methods.

```
emp := Employee{
    Person:    Person{Name: "Alice", Age: 30},
    Position: "Developer",
    Salary:   80000,
}

fmt.Println(emp.Name)  // Output: Alice (inherited from Person)
```

The embedded Person struct is automatically promoted, meaning you can access its fields and methods directly from the Employee struct.

2. Interface Embedding

Interfaces can also be embedded into other interfaces. This allows you to build more complex interfaces by composing smaller, more focused interfaces.

```
type Worker interface {
    Work()
}
```

```go
type Speaker interface {
    Speak()
}

type Employee interface {
    Worker
    Speaker
}
```

Here, Employee automatically includes all the methods defined by Worker and Speaker.

In this chapter, we explored three key features of Go: structs, methods, and interfaces. Structs provide a way to define custom data types that represent real-world entities, methods allow you to attach behavior to structs, and interfaces provide a way to define abstract types that enable polymorphism and flexible program design.

By mastering these concepts, you can create clean, modular, and reusable code in Go. Structs, methods, and interfaces are essential for building complex applications, whether you're modeling data structures, implementing behaviors, or creating abstract interfaces for extensible systems.

In the next chapter, we'll dive into **Go's concurrency model**, where we'll explore how Go makes concurrent programming simple and effective using goroutines and channels.

Go's Concurrency Model: Goroutines and Channels

One of Go's most powerful features is its built-in support for **concurrency**, which allows you to perform multiple tasks simultaneously. Go was designed with concurrency in mind from the start, and it provides simple yet powerful tools like **goroutines** and **channels** to help developers write efficient, concurrent programs with ease. Unlike traditional threading models, Go's concurrency model focuses on **lightweight, efficient parallelism** that makes it easy to write scalable applications.

In this chapter, we'll explore Go's concurrency model, focusing on **goroutines** and **channels**, which allow communication and synchronization between concurrent tasks.

Understanding Concurrency vs Parallelism

Before diving into goroutines and channels, it's important to understand the distinction between **concurrency** and **parallelism**:

- **Concurrency** is when multiple tasks are executed independently, but not necessarily at the same time. The tasks may run in an overlapping manner, sharing the same resources like CPU time.
- **Parallelism** is when multiple tasks are executed simultaneously on multiple cores or processors.

Go's concurrency model is primarily about concurrency—allowing many tasks to be written in a way that makes them independent of each other. However, when run on multi-core processors, Go can also achieve parallelism.

Goroutines: Lightweight Concurrent Functions

A **goroutine** is a function that runs concurrently with other functions. It's the fundamental building block of concurrency in Go. Unlike traditional threads in other programming languages, goroutines are lightweight and require very little overhead, allowing you to create thousands or even millions of goroutines without consuming a lot of memory.

1. Starting a Goroutine

To start a goroutine, simply use the go keyword before a function call. This tells Go to execute the function concurrently as a goroutine.

```
func sayHello() {
    fmt.Println("Hello!")
}

func main() {
    go sayHello()  // This starts a new goroutine
    fmt.Println("Main function")
}
```

In this example, the sayHello function is started as a goroutine. The main program continues to run concurrently, and both the sayHello goroutine and the main function are executed concurrently. However, since goroutines run asynchronously, you may not see "Hello!" printed if the main function exits before the goroutine has a chance to run.

2. Goroutines Are Non-blocking

Goroutines run asynchronously, which means that when a goroutine is started, the program does not wait for it to finish. This is a key difference from regular function calls, which are blocking (i.e., the program waits for the function to return before proceeding).

```
go someFunction()  // Non-blocking, continues execution
immediately
```

3. Anonymous Goroutines

You can also start a goroutine using an **anonymous function**, which allows you to define and run a function concurrently without naming it:

```
go func() {
    fmt.Println("Hello from an anonymous goroutine!")
}()
```

This creates and starts a goroutine that prints the message, all in one step.

4. Goroutines and Synchronization

One challenge with goroutines is that they are non-blocking, which means the main program may exit before the goroutines finish their work. To ensure that all goroutines complete before the program exits, you can use synchronization mechanisms such as **WaitGroups** or **channels**, which we'll cover later in this chapter.

Channels: Communication Between Goroutines

Goroutines allow you to run functions concurrently, but how do these functions communicate and share data safely? This is where **channels** come in. Channels in Go provide a way for goroutines to communicate with each other by sending and receiving values. They are a key part of Go's concurrency model and enable you to build safe, concurrent programs without the need for complex locking mechanisms.

1. Declaring and Using Channels

You declare a channel using the chan keyword, followed by the type of data that the channel will transmit. Channels can only send and receive values of a single type.

```
var messages chan string  // A channel for sending and receiving
strings
```

To create a channel, use the make function:

```
messages = make(chan string)
```

Now you can send and receive values through the channel. To send a value to the channel, use the <- operator:

```
go func() {
    messages <- "Hello from a goroutine"
}()
```

This sends the string "Hello from a goroutine" to the messages channel. To receive a value from the channel, use the <- operator again:

```
msg := <-messages
fmt.Println(msg)  // Output: Hello from a goroutine
```

In this example, the main function waits until a value is sent to the messages channel, retrieves it, and prints it.

2. Blocking Behavior of Channels

Channels are **blocking** by default. When a goroutine sends a value on a channel, it waits until another goroutine receives that value. Similarly, a goroutine that receives from a channel will wait until a value is sent.

```
messages := make(chan string)

go func() {
    messages <- "Hello"
}()
```

```
msg := <-messages   // The main goroutine waits until a message is
received
fmt.Println(msg)
```

This blocking behavior simplifies synchronization between goroutines. You don't need to use mutexes or other synchronization primitives—just use channels to synchronize the sending and receiving of data.

3. Buffered Channels

By default, channels are **unbuffered**, meaning they only hold a single value at a time. If you need a channel that can hold multiple values, you can create a **buffered channel** by specifying the buffer size when calling make.

```
messages := make(chan string, 2)   // A channel that can hold 2
messages
```

In this example, you can send two values to the messages channel without blocking:

```
messages <- "Hello"
messages <- "World"

fmt.Println(<-messages)   // Output: Hello
fmt.Println(<-messages)   // Output: World
```

With buffered channels, the sender can send values to the channel until the buffer is full. Once the buffer is full, the sender will block until a value is received from the channel.

4. Closing Channels

You can close a channel to signal that no more values will be sent. This is useful in cases where you need to inform the receiver that no more data will be transmitted.

```
close(messages)
```

Receivers can detect when a channel is closed using a second value returned by the <- operator:

```
msg, ok := <-messages
if !ok {
    fmt.Println("Channel is closed")
}
```

The ok value will be false if the channel is closed and all values have been received.

Select: Multiplexing Channels

Go provides the select statement, which allows you to wait on multiple channel operations. It's similar to a switch statement, but for channels. The select statement blocks until one of the channel operations can proceed, making it a powerful tool for building concurrent systems that need to handle multiple inputs.

1. Using Select with Channels

Here's an example of how to use select to wait on multiple channels:

```
func main() {
    c1 := make(chan string)
    c2 := make(chan string)

    go func() {
        c1 <- "Message from c1"
    }()

    go func() {
        c2 <- "Message from c2"
    }()

    select {
    case msg1 := <-c1:
        fmt.Println("Received:", msg1)
    case msg2 := <-c2:
```

```
        fmt.Println("Received:", msg2)
    }
}
```

In this example, the select statement waits until a value is available on either c1 or c2, then prints the received value. The select statement allows you to handle multiple channels in a non-blocking way.

2. Default Case in Select

You can add a **default case** to a select statement to handle cases where none of the channels are ready to communicate. The default case is executed immediately if no other cases are ready.

```
select {
case msg := <-c1:
    fmt.Println("Received:", msg)
default:
    fmt.Println("No messages received")
}
```

In this example, if neither c1 nor c2 has a value to send, the default case will execute, preventing the program from blocking indefinitely.

WaitGroups: Synchronizing Goroutines

While channels are great for communication between goroutines, you sometimes need to wait for multiple goroutines to complete their work before continuing. This is where **WaitGroups** come in. WaitGroups allow you to synchronize a group of goroutines by waiting for all of them to finish.

1. Using WaitGroups

A **WaitGroup** is part of the sync package, and it provides a counter that tracks how many goroutines are running. When a goroutine finishes, it decrements the counter, and the main program waits until the counter reaches zero.

Here's how to use a WaitGroup:

```
var wg sync.WaitGroup

wg.Add(1)  // Add 1 to the WaitGroup counter

go func() {
    defer wg.Done()  // Decrement the counter when the goroutine
    completes
    fmt.Println("Goroutine finished")
}()

wg.Wait()  // Wait for all goroutines to finish
fmt.Println("All goroutines finished")
```

In this example, the main program waits until the goroutine has finished before printing the final message. The defer wg.Done() statement ensures that the counter is decremented even if the goroutine encounters an error.

2. Waiting for Multiple Goroutines

You can use WaitGroups to wait for multiple goroutines by incrementing the counter for each goroutine and calling Done when each goroutine finishes:

```
var wg sync.WaitGroup

for i := 0; i < 3; i++ {
    wg.Add(1)
    go func(i int) {
        defer wg.Done()
        fmt.Printf("Goroutine %d finished\n", i)
    }(i)
}

wg.Wait()  // Wait for all goroutines to finish
fmt.Println("All goroutines finished")
```

In this case, the main function waits for all three goroutines to complete before printing the final message.

Practical Concurrency: Building a Concurrent Web Scraper

To see goroutines and channels in action, let's build a simple concurrent web scraper. The goal is to scrape the contents of multiple websites concurrently and print the results.

Here's the code for a basic web scraper using goroutines and channels:

```go
package main

import (
    "fmt"
    "io/ioutil"
    "net/http"
)

func fetchURL(url string, results chan<- string) {
    resp, err := http.Get(url)
    if err != nil {
        results <- fmt.Sprintf("Error fetching %s: %v", url, err)
        return
    }
    defer resp.Body.Close()

    body, err := ioutil.ReadAll(resp.Body)
    if err != nil {
        results <- fmt.Sprintf("Error reading response from %s:
        %v", url, err)
        return
    }
    results <- fmt.Sprintf("Fetched %d bytes from %s", len(body),
    url)
}

func main() {
    urls := []string{
        "https://example.com",
        "https://golang.org",
        "https://google.com",
    }
```

```
    results := make(chan string)
    for _, url := range urls {
        go fetchURL(url, results)
    }

    for range urls {
        fmt.Println(<-results)
    }
}
```

In this example:

- We define a fetchURL function that fetches the content of a URL and sends the result to a channel.
- We start a goroutine for each URL to fetch the contents concurrently.
- The main function collects and prints the results from the results channel.

This program demonstrates how to use goroutines and channels to perform multiple tasks concurrently and synchronize their results.

Go's concurrency model, built around **goroutines** and **channels**, provides an easy-to-use, efficient way to write concurrent programs. Goroutines allow you to run functions concurrently with minimal overhead, and channels enable safe communication between them. By using **select** and **WaitGroups**, you can synchronize and manage goroutines effectively, building scalable and robust applications.

In this chapter, you've learned the fundamentals of Go's concurrency model, including how to start goroutines, communicate between them using channels, and synchronize them with WaitGroups. In the next chapter, we'll dive into **optimizing performance in Go**, exploring ways to write high-performance Go programs by leveraging Go's concurrency, memory management, and profiling tools.

Packages and Go Modules

One of Go's core design principles is simplicity and efficiency, and this extends to how code is organized and managed. Go uses **packages** and **modules** to help you structure, organize, and manage your code, dependencies, and projects. Packages allow you to break up your code into reusable and maintainable units, while modules make it easy to manage dependencies and versions, ensuring that your project remains consistent across different environments and over time.

In this chapter, we'll explore how to define and use packages, work with Go modules, and understand dependency management in Go. By the end of this chapter, you'll be able to structure Go applications cleanly and manage external libraries effectively.

What Are Packages in Go?

A **package** in Go is a collection of related Go source files that are grouped together to form reusable code. Packages allow you to organize your code into modular components, making it easier to manage large applications. Every Go source file belongs to a package, and the package name is declared at the top of the file.

1. Declaring a Package

To declare a package in Go, use the package keyword followed by the package name. For example:

```
package main
```

Every Go program starts with the main package. The main package is special because Go programs always start executing from the main function in the main package. However, Go programs can import other packages that define functionality, making the main package a coordination point for larger applications.

2. Creating Custom Packages

Go encourages you to create your own packages to organize your code. A custom package is defined in its own directory, and every Go file in that directory belongs to the same package.

Here's how you create a simple custom package:

1. Create a directory for your package, for example, mathutil.
2. Create a Go file inside that directory, say mathutil.go, and declare the package name:

```
package mathutil

// Add two numbers and return the result
func Add(a, b int) int {
    return a + b
}
```

The Add function is now part of the mathutil package. To use this package, you must import it in the main package (or any other package).

1. Use your custom package in the main package:

```
package main

import (
    "fmt"
    "path/to/your/mathutil"  // Replace with the actual import
```

```
    path
)

func main() {
    result := mathutil.Add(3, 4)
    fmt.Println("Result:", result)
}
```

3. Exporting Symbols

In Go, only **exported** symbols (functions, variables, types, etc.) can be accessed by code outside of the package they are defined in. Symbols are exported if their names start with an **uppercase letter**.

For example, in the mathutil package, the Add function is exported because it starts with an uppercase letter. If it were named add, it would not be accessible outside the package.

```
// Exported function (accessible outside the package)
func Add(a, b int) int {
    return a + b
}

// Unexported function (not accessible outside the package)
func subtract(a, b int) int {
    return a - b
}
```

Exporting only what you need helps maintain encapsulation and makes your packages easier to use and maintain.

4. Organizing Code into Packages

As your projects grow, you'll want to organize your code into multiple packages to improve modularity and reusability. For example, you might organize a project like this:

```
project/
    main.go         // Main program entry point
```

```
mathutil/       // Utility functions for mathematical
operations
    mathutil.go
stringutil/     // Utility functions for string operations
    stringutil.go
```

Each directory represents a package, and the main package imports the other packages as needed.

Standard Library Packages

Go's **standard library** includes a wide variety of packages that provide essential functionality, ranging from input/output operations to cryptography. You can import and use any of these packages without needing to install external dependencies.

1. Commonly Used Standard Packages

Some of the most commonly used packages in the Go standard library include:

- **fmt**: Provides formatted I/O functions, such as fmt.Println for printing to the console.
- **os**: Provides functions to work with the operating system, such as reading and writing files, and interacting with environment variables.
- **io**: Provides basic input/output primitives, such as readers and writers.
- **net/http**: Provides HTTP client and server implementations, useful for building web applications and interacting with web services.
- **time**: Provides functions for working with dates, times, and time durations.
- **strings**: Provides utility functions for manipulating and working with strings.

For example, here's how to import and use the fmt package:

```
package main

import "fmt"

func main() {
    fmt.Println("Hello, World!")
}
```

The standard library's packages are well-documented, stable, and optimized for performance, making them a crucial resource for Go developers.

Understanding Go Modules

In Go, **modules** provide a way to manage dependencies and version control for your projects. A Go module is essentially a collection of Go packages that are versioned together and can be shared with other developers. The introduction of Go modules in Go 1.11 revolutionized dependency management, making it easier to handle dependencies without the need for a centralized workspace.

1. Initializing a New Go Module

To initialize a new Go module, you use the go mod init command. This command creates a go.mod file, which serves as the configuration file for your module. It tracks the module's dependencies and their versions.

Here's how to initialize a Go module:

1. Open a terminal and navigate to your project's directory.
2. Run the following command:

```
go mod init example.com/myproject
```

Replace example.com/myproject with the appropriate module path for your project. This creates a go.mod file in the root directory of your project.

2. The go.mod File

The go.mod file contains metadata about your module, including the module path and the required dependencies. Here's an example of a simple go.mod file:

```
module example.com/myproject

go 1.17

require (
    github.com/sirupsen/logrus v1.8.1
)
```

The module directive specifies the module's name, and the require directive lists the dependencies, including the exact version that your project depends on.

3. Adding and Managing Dependencies

To add a dependency to your Go module, you can use the go get command. For example, to add the popular logrus logging package to your project, run the following command:

```
go get github.com/sirupsen/logrus
```

This command adds logrus as a dependency and updates the go.mod file to reflect the new requirement.

Go modules automatically handle versioning and will fetch the appropriate version of a package from its repository.

4. The go.sum File

In addition to the go.mod file, Go creates a go.sum file that records the cryptographic hashes of the exact versions of dependencies you're using. This ensures the integrity of your project's dependencies and allows Go to verify that the correct version of each package is used.

Here's an example of a go.sum file:

```
github.com/sirupsen/logrus v1.8.1 h1:abc123...
github.com/sirupsen/logrus v1.8.1/go.mod h1:def456...
```

The go.sum file helps ensure that your project remains consistent across different environments, preventing issues caused by unexpected changes in dependencies.

5. Updating and Removing Dependencies

You can update a dependency to its latest version using the go get command:

```
go get -u github.com/sirupsen/logrus
```

The -u flag tells Go to fetch the latest available version of the dependency. Go automatically updates the go.mod and go.sum files to reflect the changes.

To remove a dependency, simply delete all references to the package in your code and run the following command:

```
go mod tidy
```

This command removes any unused dependencies from the go.mod file, keeping your project clean and up-to-date.

Working with Multiple Modules

Go modules provide a powerful way to manage dependencies across multiple projects. When working on large projects, you may want to break your code into multiple modules, each with its own go.mod file. This approach allows you to version and release each module independently, giving you more control over your codebase.

1. Requiring Other Modules

To use another module in your project, simply import it in your code and run go mod tidy. Go will automatically download the required module and add it to your go.mod file.

For example, if you're working on a project that depends on another module hosted at github.com/user/util, you can import the module like this:

```
import "github.com/user/util"
```

After importing the module, run go mod tidy to update your dependencies.

2. Releasing Your Own Module

When you're ready to release your Go module, you can push your code to a public repository (e.g., GitHub, GitLab). Other developers can then import and use your module in their projects by including the module path in their go.mod file.

To version your module, use **semantic versioning**. For example, you can tag a new release by running:

```
git tag v1.0.0
git push origin v1.0.0
```

Once your module is versioned, other projects can specify the version they want to use in their go.mod file, ensuring that they always get the correct version.

Best Practices for Go Packages and Modules

Here are some best practices to keep in mind when working with Go packages and modules:

1. Keep Packages Small and Focused

Each package should have a clear responsibility and should focus on a single piece of functionality. For example, don't mix database code with HTTP handlers in the same package. Use descriptive package names that reflect the package's purpose.

2. Use Consistent Naming Conventions

Follow Go's naming conventions for package names and function names. Package names should be all lowercase, and function names should start with an uppercase letter if they need to be exported. Keep names concise and meaningful.

3. Minimize the Use of Global Variables

Global variables can lead to tightly coupled code, making it harder to test and maintain. Instead, use dependency injection and pass dependencies explicitly between functions and packages.

4. Version Your Modules

When developing libraries or shared code, use semantic versioning (v1.0.0, v2.0.0, etc.) to make it easier for others to use your module. Always communicate breaking changes through major version increments.

5. Document Your Packages

Provide clear and concise documentation for your packages and modules. Use Go's built-in documentation system by adding comments to exported functions, structs, and types. You can generate documentation using the go doc command or tools like godoc.

In this chapter, we explored how Go organizes code using **packages** and **modules**, two foundational concepts for structuring and managing Go projects. You learned how to create custom packages, manage dependencies with Go modules, and use the go.mod file to track and version your project's dependencies. With this knowledge, you're well-equipped to structure your Go projects in a modular, maintainable way, making your code more reusable and easier to manage.

In the next chapter, we'll dive into **testing and debugging** in Go, where you'll learn how to write unit tests, benchmark your code, and effectively debug your Go programs.

Testing and Debugging in Go

Testing and debugging are critical parts of software development. They ensure that your code behaves as expected and help you find and fix issues quickly. Go comes with robust, built-in support for **unit testing**, **benchmarking**, and **debugging**, making it easy for developers to write reliable code and improve performance.

In this chapter, we'll cover Go's built-in testing tools, how to write effective unit tests, work with benchmarks, and use debugging techniques to troubleshoot issues. By mastering these techniques, you'll be able to improve the quality of your Go code and ensure it performs optimally.

Writing Unit Tests in Go

Go has built-in support for writing and running tests. Unit testing in Go is done using the testing package, which provides functions and methods to create test cases for your code. Tests in Go are typically written in the same package as the code they test and follow specific naming conventions.

1. Writing Your First Test

To create a test file, name it with the suffix _test.go. For example, if you're testing functions in mathutil.go, your test file should be named mathutil_test.go.

Here's a simple test for an Add function:

```
package mathutil
```

```
import "testing"

// Add two integers
func Add(a, b int) int {
    return a + b
}

// Test function for Add
func TestAdd(t *testing.T) {
    result := Add(2, 3)
    expected := 5

    if result != expected {
        t.Errorf("Add(2, 3) = %d; want %d", result, expected)
    }
}
```

In this example:

- The TestAdd function is a unit test for the Add function.
- It uses the *testing.T type, which is passed to each test function, allowing you to log errors or fail the test if needed.
- The t.Errorf function is used to report a test failure if the result doesn't match the expected value.

2. Running Tests

To run your tests, use the go test command from the command line:

```
go test
```

Go automatically detects all test files (files that end with _test.go) and runs any test functions whose names start with Test. If your tests pass, you'll see output like this:

```
ok  mypackage0.123s
```

If a test fails, Go provides detailed output showing which test failed and why.

3. Table-Driven Tests

Go encourages the use of **table-driven tests**, which allow you to define multiple test cases in a clean, concise manner. This approach is particularly useful when testing functions with multiple inputs and expected outputs.

Here's an example of a table-driven test for the Add function:

```go
func TestAdd(t *testing.T) {
    testCases := []struct {
        a, b, expected int
    }{
        {2, 3, 5},
        {0, 0, 0},
        {-1, 1, 0},
        {10, -2, 8},
    }

    for _, tc := range testCases {
        result := Add(tc.a, tc.b)
        if result != tc.expected {
            t.Errorf("Add(%d, %d) = %d; want %d", tc.a, tc.b,
                result, tc.expected)
        }
    }
}
```

In this test, we define a table of test cases and iterate through each one, checking if the Add function returns the expected result. Table-driven tests are a powerful way to keep your tests concise and maintainable.

4. Testing for Errors

In Go, functions often return error values. When testing functions that return errors, it's important to check both the result and the error.

Here's an example of testing a division function that can return an error:

```go
func Divide(a, b float64) (float64, error) {
    if b == 0 {
```

```
        return 0, fmt.Errorf("cannot divide by zero")
    }
    return a / b, nil
}

func TestDivide(t *testing.T) {
    _, err := Divide(4, 0)
    if err == nil {
        t.Error("expected error when dividing by zero")
    }
}
```

In this test, we check whether the error returned by Divide is non-nil when dividing by zero. If no error is returned, the test fails.

Test Coverage

Test coverage measures how much of your code is exercised by your tests. Go provides a simple way to measure test coverage using the -cover flag with go test.

To run tests and measure coverage, use:

```
go test -cover
```

This command outputs the percentage of code that is covered by tests. For more detailed coverage reports, you can generate a coverage profile:

```
go test -coverprofile=coverage.out
go tool cover -html=coverage.out
```

This generates an HTML report that visually shows which lines of code are covered by tests and which are not.

Benchmarking in Go

In addition to writing tests, Go allows you to write **benchmarks** to measure the performance of your code. Benchmarks are written in a similar way to tests, but they use the *testing.B type to control how many iterations the benchmark runs.

1. Writing a Benchmark

Benchmark functions follow the naming convention BenchmarkX, where X is the name of the function you're benchmarking. They take a *testing.B argument, which controls how many times the benchmark is run.

Here's an example of a benchmark for the Add function:

```
func BenchmarkAdd(b *testing.B) {
    for i := 0; i < b.N; i++ {
        Add(2, 3)
    }
}
```

In this benchmark, the b.N value determines how many iterations the benchmark should run. Go automatically increases b.N to get more accurate measurements.

2. Running Benchmarks

To run benchmarks, use the -bench flag with go test:

```
go test -bench=.
```

This runs all the benchmarks in your package and reports the time taken to execute each one. The output looks like this:

```
BenchmarkAdd-8    2000000000         0.25 ns/op
```

This means that the Add function was benchmarked 2 billion times, and each iteration took an average of 0.25 nanoseconds.

3. Benchmarking Best Practices

Here are some best practices for writing benchmarks:

- **Avoid IO in Benchmarks**: IO operations like reading files or making network requests can distort benchmark results. Focus on CPU-bound tasks.

- **Preallocate Data**: Ensure that any data used in the benchmark is preallocated outside the loop to avoid measuring setup overhead.
- **Compare Different Approaches**: Use benchmarks to compare different implementations of the same functionality and optimize performance.

Debugging in Go

Debugging is a crucial part of development, and Go provides several tools and techniques to help you identify and fix issues in your code.

1. Printing Values (Debugging with fmt)

The simplest way to debug in Go is to print values to the console using the fmt package. While this method is straightforward, it's not always the most efficient way to find and fix issues, especially in large programs.

```
fmt.Println("Value of x:", x)
```

Use this approach sparingly, as it can clutter your code and be difficult to manage in large-scale debugging efforts.

2. Using panic and recover for Debugging

Go provides the panic and recover mechanisms for handling and debugging unexpected conditions. panic immediately stops the normal execution flow and begins unwinding the stack, while recover allows you to regain control after a panic.

Here's how you might use panic for debugging:

```
if x == 0 {
    panic("unexpected zero value")
}
```

This stops execution immediately if the condition is met, allowing you to see where the issue occurred.

However, panic should only be used for debugging or handling truly exceptional conditions. In most cases, you should prefer handling errors with the standard error return values.

3. Debugging with Delve

Delve is the official debugger for Go. It provides a powerful way to inspect your program's state, set breakpoints, and step through code during execution.

To install Delve, use the following command:

```
go install github.com/go-delve/delve/cmd/dlv@latest
```

Once installed, you can start debugging a program by running:

```
dlv debug main.go
```

This starts your program in debug mode. You can then set breakpoints, inspect variables, and step through the code using commands like break, next, print, and continue.

4. Example Delve Commands

- **Set a breakpoint**: break main.go:10 (sets a breakpoint at line 10 in main.go).
- **Continue execution**: continue (continues running the program until the next breakpoint).
- **Print a variable's value**: print x (prints the value of x at the current execution point).
- **Step through code**: next (steps to the next line of code).

Delve is a powerful tool for debugging complex issues, as it allows you to control the execution flow and inspect the internal state of your program.

Profiling in Go

Profiling helps you understand where your program spends most of its time or uses the most memory. Go's built-in profiling tools can be used to identify bottlenecks and optimize your code.

1. CPU Profiling

You can enable CPU profiling by using the pprof package. Here's how to add CPU profiling to your code:

```go
import (
    "os"
    "runtime/pprof"
)

func main() {
    f, _ := os.Create("cpu.prof")
    pprof.StartCPUProfile(f)
    defer pprof.StopCPUProfile()

    // Your program code here
}
```

Run your program, and it generates a cpu.prof file that contains profiling data. You can analyze this data using the go tool pprof command:

```
go tool pprof cpu.prof
```

Once inside pprof, you can use commands like top to see the top CPU-consuming functions and list to view the source code with annotated performance data.

2. Memory Profiling

To profile memory usage, you can use the pprof package in a similar way:

```go
import (
    "os"
    "runtime/pprof"
)

func main() {
```

```
    f, _ := os.Create("mem.prof")
    pprof.WriteHeapProfile(f)
    f.Close()

    // Your program code here
}
```

This generates a mem.prof file that you can analyze with go tool pprof to identify memory usage patterns and potential memory leaks.

Testing, debugging, and profiling are essential skills for writing high-quality, performant Go programs. In this chapter, you learned how to write unit tests, measure test coverage, benchmark your code, and debug issues using both simple print statements and more advanced tools like Delve. You also learned how to use profiling to identify performance bottlenecks.

By mastering these tools and techniques, you'll be able to write reliable, maintainable, and efficient Go code. In the next chapter, we'll explore **performance optimization in Go**, diving deeper into how to write high-performance Go applications by leveraging concurrency, efficient data structures, and optimized algorithms.

Building Web Applications with Go

Go has become a popular choice for building web applications due to its simplicity, efficiency, and built-in support for concurrency. With a powerful standard library, Go allows you to build scalable web servers without relying on heavy frameworks. Whether you're creating a small API or a large web application, Go's robust performance, concurrency model, and straightforward syntax make it a powerful tool for web development.

In this chapter, we'll explore how to build web applications with Go, including how to create web servers, handle routing, manage middleware, and work with templates. By the end of this chapter, you'll have a solid foundation for building web applications in Go.

Getting Started with HTTP in Go

At the core of Go's web capabilities is the net/http package, which provides the tools you need to create web servers, handle requests and responses, and serve content over HTTP. The net/http package is included in Go's standard library, so there is no need to install any external dependencies.

1. Creating a Simple Web Server

The simplest web server in Go is just a few lines of code. You use the http.HandleFunc function to define routes and the http.ListenAndServe function to start the server.

```go
package main

import (
    "fmt"
    "net/http"
)

func handler(w http.ResponseWriter, r *http.Request) {
    fmt.Fprintf(w, "Hello, World!")
}

func main() {
    http.HandleFunc("/", handler)      // Define a route
    http.ListenAndServe(":8080", nil)  // Start the server on
    port 8080
}
```

In this example:

- The handler function processes requests. It writes the response "Hello, World!" to the http.ResponseWriter, which is used to send responses back to the client.
- http.HandleFunc("/", handler) sets up a route for the root URL (/) and associates it with the handler function.
- http.ListenAndServe(":8080", nil) starts the web server on port 8080. The server listens for incoming requests and directs them to the appropriate handler.

2. Handling HTTP Requests

Go's http.Request object gives you access to all the information about an HTTP request, such as the URL, method (GET, POST, etc.), headers, and query parameters. You can use this data to build dynamic responses.

Here's how to access and handle various parts of an HTTP request:

```go
func handler(w http.ResponseWriter, r *http.Request) {
    fmt.Fprintf(w, "Method: %s\n", r.Method)    // Request method
    (GET, POST, etc.)
    fmt.Fprintf(w, "URL: %s\n", r.URL.Path)      // Requested URL
    path
    fmt.Fprintf(w, "Query: %s\n", r.URL.RawQuery) // Query
    parameters
    fmt.Fprintf(w, "Headers: %v\n", r.Header)    // Request headers
}
```

This code extracts various parts of the request, such as the HTTP method, URL, query parameters, and headers, and sends them back to the client as part of the response.

3. Sending HTTP Responses

The http.ResponseWriter interface allows you to send data back to the client. You can send simple text responses or set headers and status codes.

Here's how to send different types of responses:

```go
func handler(w http.ResponseWriter, r *http.Request) {
    w.Header().Set("Content-Type", "text/plain")   // Set response
    headers
    w.WriteHeader(http.StatusOK)                    // Set status
    code (200 OK)
    fmt.Fprintln(w, "Hello, World!")                // Write the
    response body
}
```

In this example, we explicitly set the content type to text/plain, return a status code of 200 (OK), and send a text response to the client.

Routing in Go

Routing determines how your application responds to different HTTP requests. Go's net/http package provides basic routing capabilities through http.HandleFunc, but for more advanced routing features, you can use third-party libraries like **Gorilla Mux** or **Gin**.

1. Basic Routing with http.HandleFunc

In the simplest case, you can define multiple routes using http.HandleFunc:

```
func main() {
    http.HandleFunc("/", homeHandler)       // Route for the
    homepage
    http.HandleFunc("/about", aboutHandler) // Route for the
    about page

    http.ListenAndServe(":8080", nil)  // Start the server
}
```

Each route is associated with a handler function that responds to requests for that particular path.

2. Using Gorilla Mux for Advanced Routing

For more advanced routing, you can use **Gorilla Mux**, a powerful, flexible router for Go. Gorilla Mux allows you to define routes with URL parameters, handle methods more easily, and implement more complex routing patterns.

To install Gorilla Mux, run the following command:

```
go get -u github.com/gorilla/mux
```

Here's how to set up basic routes with Gorilla Mux:

```
package main

import (
    "fmt"
    "net/http"
    "github.com/gorilla/mux"
)

func homeHandler(w http.ResponseWriter, r *http.Request) {
    fmt.Fprintln(w, "Welcome to the homepage!")
}

func productHandler(w http.ResponseWriter, r *http.Request) {
```

```
    vars := mux.Vars(r)  // Extract URL parameters
    fmt.Fprintf(w, "Product ID: %s\n", vars["id"])
}

func main() {
    r := mux.NewRouter()
    r.HandleFunc("/", homeHandler)
    r.HandleFunc("/product/{id}", productHandler) // Route with
    URL parameter

    http.ListenAndServe(":8080", r)
}
```

In this example:

- mux.NewRouter() creates a new router.
- We define a route with a URL parameter (/product/{id}), which captures the product ID from the URL.
- The mux.Vars(r) function extracts the URL parameters and makes them available in the handler function.

Working with Middleware

Middleware in Go is a way to process requests and responses before or after they reach your handlers. Middleware functions allow you to add common functionality (e.g., logging, authentication, or request validation) that can be reused across different routes.

1. Creating Middleware

Here's how to create a simple logging middleware that logs each incoming request:

```
func loggingMiddleware(next http.Handler) http.Handler {
    return http.HandlerFunc(func(w http.ResponseWriter, r
    *http.Request) {
        fmt.Printf("Request: %s %s\n", r.Method, r.URL.Path)
        next.ServeHTTP(w, r)  // Call the next handler
```

```
    })
}
```

The loggingMiddleware function wraps a handler and logs the HTTP method and URL path for each request. The next.ServeHTTP(w, r) call ensures that the next handler in the chain is executed.

2. Using Middleware with Gorilla Mux

You can use middleware with Gorilla Mux by adding it to the router:

```
r := mux.NewRouter()
r.Use(loggingMiddleware)  // Add the logging middleware

r.HandleFunc("/", homeHandler)
r.HandleFunc("/about", aboutHandler)
```

Now, every request to the server will go through the logging middleware before reaching the handler.

Serving Static Files

In most web applications, you'll need to serve static assets like images, CSS files, and JavaScript files. Go's http.FileServer function makes it easy to serve static files from a directory.

Here's how to serve static files:

```
http.Handle("/static/", http.StripPrefix("/static/",
http.FileServer(http.Dir("./static"))))
```

In this example:

- http.FileServer(http.Dir("./static")) creates a file server that serves files from the ./static directory.
- http.StripPrefix("/static/", ...) removes the /static/ prefix from the URL path, ensuring that the file paths match the directory structure.

Now, files in the ./static directory can be accessed at URLs like /static/styles.css.

Rendering HTML Templates

Go provides the html/template package, which makes it easy to generate HTML content from templates. This is useful when building dynamic web pages where the content changes based on user input or data from a database.

1. Creating and Rendering Templates

Here's how to define and render a simple HTML template:

- Create an HTML file named index.html:

```html
<!DOCTYPE html>
<html>
<head>
    <title>{{ .Title }}</title>
</head>
<body>
    <h1>{{ .Title }}</h1>
    <p>{{ .Body }}</p>
</body>
</html>
```

- In your Go code, load and render the template:

```go
package main

import (
    "html/template"
    "net/http"
)
```

```go
func homeHandler(w http.ResponseWriter, r *http.Request) {
    tmpl := template.Must(template.ParseFiles("index.html"))
    data := struct {
        Title string
        Body  string
    }{
        Title: "Welcome",
        Body:  "Hello, World!",
    }
    tmpl.Execute(w, data)
}

func main() {
    http.HandleFunc("/", homeHandler)
    http.ListenAndServe(":8080", nil)
}
```

In this example:

- We use the template.Must function to parse the index.html file. This ensures the template is loaded correctly, and it panics if there is an error.
- The Execute method renders the template with the provided data and sends the output to the client.

2. Template Functions and Logic

Go templates support basic logic like conditionals and loops, allowing you to create dynamic content.

Here's an example of a template that uses a loop to render a list of items:

```html
<ul>
    {{ range .Items }}
    <li>{{ . }}</li>
    {{ end }}
</ul>
```

In Go, you pass a slice to the template to render the list:

```
data := struct {
    Items []string
}{
    Items: []string{"Item 1", "Item 2", "Item 3"},
}
tmpl.Execute(w, data)
```

The range action iterates over the slice of items, rendering each one as a list item.

Handling Forms and Processing Input

Web applications often need to handle user input through forms. Go makes it easy to process form data sent via POST requests.

1. Handling Form Submissions

Here's how to handle a simple form submission:

```
func formHandler(w http.ResponseWriter, r *http.Request) {
    if r.Method == "POST" {
        name := r.FormValue("name")   // Get form value
        email := r.FormValue("email") // Get another form value

        fmt.Fprintf(w, "Name: %s\n", name)
        fmt.Fprintf(w, "Email: %s\n", email)
    } else {
        http.Error(w, "Invalid request method",
        http.StatusMethodNotAllowed)
    }
}

func main() {
    http.HandleFunc("/submit", formHandler)
    http.ListenAndServe(":8080", nil)
}
```

In this example:

- We use r.FormValue("name") to get the value of the name field from the form.

- The handler checks if the request method is POST and then processes the form data. If the method is not POST, an error is returned.

2. Form Validation

You can easily add form validation to check for required fields or ensure that the input data is valid:

```
func formHandler(w http.ResponseWriter, r *http.Request) {
    if r.Method == "POST" {
        name := r.FormValue("name")
        email := r.FormValue("email")

        if name == "" || email == "" {
            http.Error(w, "Missing name or email",
            http.StatusBadRequest)
            return
        }

        fmt.Fprintf(w, "Name: %s\n", name)
        fmt.Fprintf(w, "Email: %s\n", email)
    }
}
```

In this example, we check if the name or email fields are empty and return an error if the validation fails.

In this chapter, we explored the essentials of building web applications with Go, covering how to create web servers, handle HTTP requests and responses, manage routing with Gorilla Mux, and render HTML templates. You also learned how to implement middleware for reusable functionality and how to handle form submissions.

Go's simplicity and efficiency make it an excellent choice for building web applications, whether you're working on a small project or a large, scalable system. With Go's concurrency model and lightweight nature, you can build high-performance web applications that handle many users efficiently.

In the next chapter, we'll dive into **working with databases in Go**, exploring how to connect to databases, perform CRUD operations, and handle transactions and connection pooling.

Working with Databases in Go

D atabases are a critical part of almost all web applications, and Go provides powerful tools to interact with them. Whether you're building a REST API or a full-stack web application, Go's standard library, along with third-party packages, makes working with databases both straightforward and efficient. This chapter will cover how to connect to databases, perform CRUD (Create, Read, Update, Delete) operations, manage database transactions, and implement best practices for handling database connections in Go.

In this chapter, we will focus on working with SQL databases using Go's built-in database/sql package, although Go can also be used with NoSQL databases like MongoDB.

Setting Up a Database Connection

Go provides the database/sql package for working with SQL databases. The package offers a generic interface that allows Go to connect to different databases using database-specific drivers. For example, for PostgreSQL, we use the pq driver, and for MySQL, we use the mysql driver.

1. Installing a Database Driver

Before connecting to a database, you need to install the appropriate driver for the database you want to use. For example, to connect to a PostgreSQL database, you can use the pq driver. To install it, run:

```
go get -u github.com/lib/pq
```

For MySQL, you can use the mysql driver:

```
go get -u github.com/go-sql-driver/mysql
```

2. Connecting to the Database

Once the driver is installed, you can connect to your database using the sql.Open function. This function takes two parameters: the driver name and the connection string.

Here's how to connect to a PostgreSQL database:

```
package main

import (
    "database/sql"
    "fmt"
    _ "github.com/lib/pq"  // Import the pq driver
)

func main() {
    connStr := "user=username dbname=mydb sslmode=disable"
    db, err := sql.Open("postgres", connStr)
    if err != nil {
        fmt.Println("Error connecting to the database:", err)
        return
    }
    defer db.Close()

    fmt.Println("Successfully connected to the database!")
}
```

For MySQL, the connection string format is slightly different:

```
package main

import (
    "database/sql"
    "fmt"
```

```
    _ "github.com/go-sql-driver/mysql"  // Import the MySQL driver
)

func main() {
    connStr := "username:password@tcp(127.0.0.1:3306)/mydb"
    db, err := sql.Open("mysql", connStr)
    if err != nil {
        fmt.Println("Error connecting to the database:", err)
        return
    }
    defer db.Close()

    fmt.Println("Successfully connected to the MySQL database!")
}
```

In both examples:

- sql.Open("postgres", connStr) or sql.Open("mysql", connStr) opens a connection to the database.
- The defer db.Close() ensures that the database connection is closed when the program exits.

Note that sql.Open does not establish a connection immediately; instead, it validates the arguments. You should use db.Ping() to verify that the connection to the database is successful:

```
err = db.Ping()
if err != nil {
    fmt.Println("Database connection error:", err)
}
```

Performing CRUD Operations

Once connected, the next step is to perform CRUD operations: Create, Read, Update, and Delete. Go's database/sql package provides several methods for executing SQL queries and handling results.

1. Creating Records (INSERT)

You can use the Exec method to insert new records into the database. The Exec method is used for SQL commands that don't return rows, such as INSERT, UPDATE, and DELETE.

Here's an example of inserting a new record into a PostgreSQL database:

```
query := `INSERT INTO users (name, email) VALUES ($1, $2)`
_, err := db.Exec(query, "Alice", "alice@example.com")
if err != nil {
    fmt.Println("Error inserting record:", err)
}
```

For MySQL, the query would look like this:

```
query := `INSERT INTO users (name, email) VALUES (?, ?)`
_, err := db.Exec(query, "Alice", "alice@example.com")
if err != nil {
    fmt.Println("Error inserting record:", err)
}
```

The Exec method takes the SQL query and the values for the placeholders ($1, $2 in PostgreSQL, and ? in MySQL).

2. Reading Records (SELECT)

To query data from the database, use the Query or QueryRow methods. Query is used for queries that return multiple rows, while QueryRow is used for queries that return a single row.

Here's how to retrieve multiple rows from a PostgreSQL database:

```
rows, err := db.Query("SELECT id, name, email FROM users")
if err != nil {
    fmt.Println("Error fetching records:", err)
    return
}
defer rows.Close()

for rows.Next() {
    var id int
```

```
    var name, email string
    err := rows.Scan(&id, &name, &email)
    if err != nil {
        fmt.Println("Error scanning record:", err)
        continue
    }
    fmt.Printf("ID: %d, Name: %s, Email: %s\n", id, name, email)
}
```

For a single row, use QueryRow:

```
var name, email string
err := db.QueryRow("SELECT name, email FROM users WHERE id = $1",
1).Scan(&name, &email)
if err != nil {
    fmt.Println("Error fetching record:", err)
} else {
    fmt.Printf("Name: %s, Email: %s\n", name, email)
}
```

In this example:

- rows.Scan() reads the data from each row into the specified variables.
- QueryRow().Scan() reads the data from a single row.

3. Updating Records (UPDATE)

To update records in the database, use the Exec method just like for INSERT. Here's an example of updating a record:

```
query := `UPDATE users SET email = $1 WHERE id = $2`
_, err := db.Exec(query, "newemail@example.com", 1)
if err != nil {
    fmt.Println("Error updating record:", err)
}
```

This query updates the email address of the user with ID 1.

4. Deleting Records (DELETE)

Similarly, you can delete records using the Exec method:

```
query := `DELETE FROM users WHERE id = $1`
_, err := db.Exec(query, 1)
if err != nil {
    fmt.Println("Error deleting record:", err)
}
```

This deletes the user with ID 1 from the users table.

Handling SQL Injection

SQL injection is a security vulnerability that occurs when untrusted input is included in an SQL query. Go protects against SQL injection by allowing you to use **placeholder parameters** ($1, $2 in PostgreSQL and ? in MySQL) in your SQL queries. The values are passed separately and are automatically escaped by the database driver.

For example, instead of writing:

```
query := fmt.Sprintf("SELECT name FROM users WHERE id = %d",
userID)  // Vulnerable to SQL injection
```

You should write:

```
query := "SELECT name FROM users WHERE id = $1"
db.QueryRow(query, userID).Scan(&name)
```

This approach ensures that user input cannot be executed as SQL code.

Transactions in Go

Transactions allow you to group multiple SQL operations into a single unit of work. If any operation in the transaction fails, you can roll back the entire transaction, ensuring data integrity.

1. Starting a Transaction

To start a transaction, use the db.Begin() method:

```
tx, err := db.Begin()
if err != nil {
    fmt.Println("Error starting transaction:", err)
    return
}
```

2. Executing Queries in a Transaction

Once the transaction is started, you can execute queries within the transaction using the tx.Exec or tx.Query methods. Here's an example of inserting two records in a transaction:

```
_, err = tx.Exec("INSERT INTO users (name, email) VALUES ($1,
$2)", "John", "john@example.com")
if err != nil {
    tx.Rollback()  // Roll back the transaction on error
    fmt.Println("Error inserting record:", err)
    return
}

_, err = tx.Exec("INSERT INTO users (name, email) VALUES ($1,
$2)", "Jane", "jane@example.com")
if err != nil {
    tx.Rollback()  // Roll back the transaction on error
    fmt.Println("Error inserting record:", err)
    return
}
```

3. Committing or Rolling Back a Transaction

If all queries are successful, commit the transaction:

```
err = tx.Commit()
if err != nil {
    fmt.Println("Error committing transaction:", err)
}
```

If an error occurs during any of the queries, you can roll back the transaction:

```
tx.Rollback()
```

Connection Pooling

Go's database/sql package provides connection pooling by default, which means it maintains a pool of open connections to the database that can be reused for multiple queries. This helps improve performance by avoiding the overhead of opening and closing database connections repeatedly.

1. Setting Connection Limits

You can control the number of connections in the pool using the following methods:

- db.SetMaxOpenConns(n) limits the maximum number of open connections.
- db.SetMaxIdleConns(n) limits the number of idle connections (connections not currently in use).
- db.SetConnMaxLifetime(duration) limits how long a connection can be reused.

Here's an example:

```
db.SetMaxOpenConns(10)         // Max 10 open connections
db.SetMaxIdleConns(5)          // Max 5 idle connections
db.SetConnMaxLifetime(time.Minute) // Reuse connections for up to
1 minute
```

These settings help optimize the performance of your application, especially under heavy load.

Best Practices for Working with Databases in Go

Here are some best practices to follow when working with databases in Go:

1. Always Check for Errors

Database operations can fail due to various reasons (e.g., network issues, incorrect queries). Always check for errors and handle them appropriately.

2. Close Rows and Connections

Always close rows and database connections using defer to prevent resource leaks.

```
rows, err := db.Query("SELECT * FROM users")
if err != nil {
    log.Fatal(err)
}
defer rows.Close()
```

3. Use Prepared Statements for Repeated Queries

If you're executing the same query multiple times, use **prepared statements** to optimize performance and prevent SQL injection attacks.

```
stmt, err := db.Prepare("INSERT INTO users (name, email) VALUES
($1, $2)")
if err != nil {
    log.Fatal(err)
}
defer stmt.Close()

_, err = stmt.Exec("Alice", "alice@example.com")
```

4. Use Transactions for Critical Operations

For operations that involve multiple queries or changes to multiple tables, use transactions to ensure that all changes are committed together or rolled back in case of failure.

5. Connection Pooling

Optimize connection pooling to improve performance by setting appropriate limits on open and idle connections, especially in high-traffic environments.

In this chapter, we explored how to work with databases in Go, including connecting to databases, performing CRUD operations, managing SQL transactions, and handling SQL injection. You also learned how to use connection pooling to optimize database performance and implement best practices for database management in Go.

With Go's built-in database/sql package and third-party drivers, you can efficiently interact with databases, whether you're building simple web applications or large-scale systems with complex data requirements.

In the next chapter, we'll dive into **building RESTful APIs with Go**, where you'll learn how to design and implement RESTful endpoints, handle JSON data, and implement common API features like authentication and rate limiting.

Advanced Concurrency Patterns

Go's concurrency model, based on **goroutines** and **channels**, is one of its standout features. In Chapter 6, we explored the basics of concurrency in Go with goroutines and channels. In this chapter, we will dive into **advanced concurrency patterns** that go beyond basic goroutines, enabling you to build more scalable, efficient, and robust applications. We'll cover techniques such as **worker pools, fan-out/fan-in, select statement** patterns, **rate limiting**, and more.

By the end of this chapter, you will be equipped to design and implement highly concurrent Go applications that can handle complex workloads with ease.

Worker Pools

A **worker pool** is a concurrency pattern where a set of worker goroutines (also called "workers") process jobs from a shared queue. This pattern helps manage a high volume of work efficiently by limiting the number of goroutines running concurrently, which prevents resource exhaustion.

Creating a Basic Worker Pool

Here's how to implement a simple worker pool in Go:

1. **Define the Job and Worker Functions**:

- The **job** is a task that needs to be processed.
- A **worker** is a goroutine that continuously listens for jobs and processes

them.

```go
package main

import (
    "fmt"
    "time"
)

type Job struct {
    ID int
}

func worker(id int, jobs <-chan Job, results chan<- string) {
    for job := range jobs {
        fmt.Printf("Worker %d started job %d\n", id, job.ID)
        time.Sleep(time.Second)  // Simulate work
        fmt.Printf("Worker %d finished job %d\n", id, job.ID)
        results <- fmt.Sprintf("Job %d completed by worker %d",
        job.ID, id)
    }
}

func main() {
    jobs := make(chan Job, 10)
    results := make(chan string, 10)

    // Start 3 workers
    for w := 1; w <= 3; w++ {
        go worker(w, jobs, results)
    }

    // Send 5 jobs to the workers
    for j := 1; j <= 5; j++ {
        jobs <- Job{ID: j}
    }
    close(jobs)

    // Collect results
```

```
    for a := 1; a <= 5; a++ {
        fmt.Println(<-results)
    }
}
```

In this example:

- Three workers are created using the go worker() function, each of which listens to the jobs channel.
- Jobs are submitted to the jobs channel, and workers pick them up as they become available.
- Results are collected in the results channel and printed.

2. Controlling the Number of Workers

You can control the number of workers in your pool by adjusting the number of goroutines started. This helps you limit the amount of parallel work being done, allowing you to control CPU and memory usage effectively.

In the example above, we limited the number of workers to 3, but you can scale this up or down depending on your system's capabilities.

Fan-Out/Fan-In Concurrency Pattern

The **Fan-Out/Fan-In** pattern is useful when you need to distribute tasks across multiple goroutines (fan-out) and then gather the results from multiple goroutines (fan-in).

1. Fan-Out Example

In a fan-out pattern, one goroutine spawns multiple goroutines that perform tasks concurrently.

Here's an example where tasks are fanned out to multiple worker goroutines:

```
func fanOutTask(id int, results chan<- string) {
    time.Sleep(time.Millisecond * time.Duration(100*id))  //
```

```
        Simulate task duration
        results <- fmt.Sprintf("Task %d completed", id)
}

func main() {
    results := make(chan string, 5)

    // Fan out: start 5 tasks concurrently
    for i := 1; i <= 5; i++ {
        go fanOutTask(i, results)
    }

    // Fan in: collect the results
    for i := 1; i <= 5; i++ {
        fmt.Println(<-results)
    }
}
```

In this example, multiple tasks are run concurrently, and their results are collected in the results channel.

2. Fan-In Example

In a fan-in pattern, you collect results from multiple channels into a single channel. Here's an example:

```
func producer(id int, out chan<- int) {
    for i := 0; i < 3; i++ {
        out <- id * 100 + i
        time.Sleep(time.Millisecond * 100)
    }
}

func main() {
    out1 := make(chan int)
    out2 := make(chan int)

    go producer(1, out1)
    go producer(2, out2)
```

```
    // Fan-in: collect data from both channels
    for i := 0; i < 6; i++ {
        select {
        case result := <-out1:
            fmt.Printf("Received from out1: %d\n", result)
        case result := <-out2:
            fmt.Printf("Received from out2: %d\n", result)
        }
    }
}
```

Here, the fan-in pattern is achieved using the select statement, which listens to multiple channels simultaneously and processes data as soon as it becomes available.

Using the Select Statement

The **select** statement in Go is used to wait on multiple channel operations. It lets you process whichever channel receives data first, making it ideal for handling multiple concurrent operations.

1. Basic Select Usage

The select statement allows a goroutine to wait on multiple communication operations. Here's a basic example:

```
func main() {
    ch1 := make(chan string)
    ch2 := make(chan string)

    go func() {
        time.Sleep(1 * time.Second)
        ch1 <- "Message from ch1"
    }()

    go func() {
        time.Sleep(2 * time.Second)
        ch2 <- "Message from ch2"
    }()
```

```
for i := 0; i < 2; i++ {
    select {
    case msg1 := <-ch1:
        fmt.Println("Received:", msg1)
    case msg2 := <-ch2:
        fmt.Println("Received:", msg2)
    }
  }
}
```

In this example:

- The program waits for messages from either ch1 or ch2. Whichever channel receives data first is processed by the select statement.

2. Using Default Case in Select

The default case in a select statement allows you to execute code when none of the channels are ready. This is useful for non-blocking channel operations.

```
select {
case msg := <-ch1:
    fmt.Println("Received from ch1:", msg)
case msg := <-ch2:
    fmt.Println("Received from ch2:", msg)
default:
    fmt.Println("No messages received")
}
```

Here, the program prints "No messages received" if neither ch1 nor ch2 is ready to send data.

Rate Limiting

Rate limiting is a common requirement in web applications and APIs to prevent overloading a system. In Go, you can implement rate limiting using channels and time-based patterns like **ticks** and **timers**.

1. Simple Rate Limiting

You can use the time.Tick function to limit how frequently a task is performed.

```go
func main() {
    requests := make(chan int, 5)
    for i := 1; i <= 5; i++ {
        requests <- i
    }
    close(requests)

    limiter := time.Tick(200 * time.Millisecond)  // Limit to one
    request every 200ms

    for req := range requests {
        <-limiter
        fmt.Println("Processing request", req, "at", time.Now())
    }
}
```

In this example:

- A time.Tick creates a ticker that fires every 200 milliseconds.
- For each request, we block until the ticker allows us to proceed.

2. Bursty Rate Limiting

You can also implement a **bursty** rate limiter that allows short bursts of requests before enforcing a slower rate.

```go
func main() {
    requests := make(chan int, 5)
    for i := 1; i <= 5; i++ {
        requests <- i
    }
```

```go
    close(requests)

    limiter := time.Tick(200 * time.Millisecond)

    burstyLimiter := make(chan time.Time, 3)  // Allow up to 3
    requests in a burst
    for i := 0; i < 3; i++ {
        burstyLimiter <- time.Now()
    }

    go func() {
        for t := range limiter {
            burstyLimiter <- t
        }
    }()

    for req := range requests {
        <-burstyLimiter
        fmt.Println("Processing request", req, "at", time.Now())
    }
}
```

In this example, the burstyLimiter allows up to three requests to be processed immediately before falling back to the rate-limited pattern.

Context for Managing Cancellation

Go's context package provides a powerful way to manage timeouts, cancellation, and deadlines for goroutines. This is particularly useful in concurrent applications where you need to control the lifecycle of goroutines and prevent them from running indefinitely.

1. Using Context for Cancellation

You can use context.WithCancel to propagate cancellation signals to goroutines:

```go
func worker(ctx context.Context, id int) {
    for {
```

```
        select {
        case <-ctx.Done():
            fmt.Printf("Worker %d stopping\n", id)
            return
        default:
            fmt.Printf("Worker %d working\n", id)
            time.Sleep(500 * time.Millisecond)
        }
    }
}

func main() {
    ctx, cancel := context.WithCancel(context.Background())

    for i := 1; i <= 3; i++ {
        go worker(ctx, i)
    }

    time.Sleep(2 * time.Second)
    cancel()  // Cancel all workers
    time.Sleep(1 * time.Second)
}
```

In this example:

- We create a cancellable context using context.WithCancel.
- The workers listen for the cancellation signal using ctx.Done().
- When cancel() is called, all workers stop their execution.

2. Timeout and Deadline Contexts

You can also set timeouts or deadlines for goroutines:

```
func main() {
    ctx, cancel := context.WithTimeout(context.Background(),
    2*time.Second)
    defer cancel()
```

```
select {
case <-time.After(3 * time.Second):
    fmt.Println("Operation completed")
case <-ctx.Done():
    fmt.Println("Timeout:", ctx.Err())
}
}
```

Here, the context.WithTimeout function creates a context that automatically cancels after 2 seconds.

In this chapter, we explored advanced concurrency patterns in Go, including **worker pools, fan-out/fan-in**, the **select** statement, **rate limiting**, and the use of **context** for managing goroutine lifecycles. These patterns help you design more scalable, efficient, and robust concurrent applications, allowing you to handle high levels of concurrency in a clean and controlled manner.

By mastering these advanced concurrency techniques, you'll be well-equipped to tackle complex problems in Go that require managing multiple tasks, coordinating communication between goroutines, and ensuring that resources are used efficiently.

In the next chapter, we'll dive into **working with Go's reflection and type system**, exploring how Go allows you to manipulate types at runtime and work with dynamic data in a type-safe manner.

Optimizing Go for Performance

P erformance optimization is a key concern when building software, especially in a language like Go, which is designed to be fast and efficient. Go's simplicity and low-level capabilities, along with its robust concurrency model, make it a great choice for building high-performance applications. However, writing performant Go code often requires a deep understanding of the language's memory management, concurrency model, and best practices for profiling and optimization.

In this chapter, we'll explore various techniques and strategies to optimize Go applications for performance. Topics will include identifying bottlenecks using profiling tools, optimizing memory usage, minimizing allocations, improving concurrency efficiency, and leveraging Go's garbage collector effectively.

1. Profiling: Identifying Bottlenecks

Before optimizing your Go application, you need to identify the parts of the code that are causing performance issues. **Profiling** is the process of measuring where your program spends most of its time or consumes the most resources.

1.1 CPU Profiling

CPU profiling helps you identify which parts of your program are using the most CPU time. Go's pprof package is a built-in tool that lets you generate CPU profiles for your application.

To start CPU profiling, add the following code to your program:

```
import (
    "os"
    "runtime/pprof"
)

func main() {
    f, _ := os.Create("cpu.prof")
    pprof.StartCPUProfile(f)
    defer pprof.StopCPUProfile()

    // Your program code here
}
```

After running your program, you can analyze the profile using the go tool pprof command:

```
go tool pprof cpu.prof
```

Inside the pprof tool, you can use commands like top to see the most time-consuming functions, or list to view annotated source code.

1.2 Memory Profiling

Memory profiling helps you understand how your program is using memory and where allocations are happening. To generate a memory profile, use the following code:

```
import (
    "os"
    "runtime/pprof"
)

func main() {
    f, _ := os.Create("mem.prof")
    pprof.WriteHeapProfile(f)
    f.Close()

    // Your program code here
```

```
}
```

After generating the mem.prof file, use go tool pprof to analyze memory usage and find potential leaks or areas of high allocation.

1.3 Benchmarking with testing.B

In addition to profiling, Go provides a built-in benchmarking tool using the testing package. You can write benchmarks to measure the performance of individual functions and optimize them accordingly.

Here's an example of a simple benchmark function:

```
import "testing"

func BenchmarkAdd(b *testing.B) {
    for i := 0; i < b.N; i++ {
        Add(2, 3)
    }
}
```

You can run benchmarks using:

```
go test -bench=.
```

The benchmark results show how long it takes to execute the function and how many iterations are performed.

2. Memory Management and Allocation Optimization

Memory management is critical to performance in Go, especially since Go's garbage collector (GC) can impact application performance if not managed carefully. Understanding how Go handles memory and how to minimize allocations can lead to significant performance gains.

2.1 Minimizing Allocations

Each time your Go program allocates memory (e.g., for new objects or slices), it adds overhead and pressure on the garbage collector. To optimize memory usage, aim to minimize unnecessary allocations.

- **Use Value Types Instead of Pointers**: In many cases, using value types (e.g., passing structs by value instead of pointers) reduces the number of allocations on the heap.
- Example:

```
type Point struct {
    X, Y int
}

// Pass by value
func Move(p Point) Point {
    p.X += 1
    p.Y += 1
    return p
}
```

- This avoids heap allocations, as the Point struct is allocated on the stack.
- **Preallocate Slices**: When working with slices, always preallocate memory using the make function to avoid multiple allocations as the slice grows.

```
s := make([]int, 0, 100)  // Preallocate capacity for 100 elements
```

- This reduces the number of reallocations when the slice grows.
- **Use Sync.Pool for Object Reuse**: Go's sync.Pool is a useful tool for reusing objects, such as large structs, across multiple requests or operations. This can reduce memory churn and garbage collection overhead.

```go
var pool = sync.Pool{
    New: func() interface{} {
        return &SomeStruct{}
    },
}

obj := pool.Get().(*SomeStruct)
// Use obj
pool.Put(obj)  // Return object to the pool for reuse
```

2.2 Managing Garbage Collection

Go's garbage collector automatically reclaims memory that is no longer in use, but it can cause performance hits, especially in low-latency systems. The key to managing garbage collection efficiently is to minimize the number of allocations and reduce the pressure on the GC.

You can adjust the behavior of the garbage collector using the GOGC environment variable, which controls the GC frequency. A lower value causes the GC to run more often, while a higher value delays GC but increases memory usage.

```
GOGC=100 go run main.go  # Default GC threshold
GOGC=200 go run main.go  # Run GC less frequently
```

3. Concurrency Optimization

Concurrency is one of Go's strengths, but writing efficient concurrent code requires understanding how to avoid common pitfalls like excessive synchronization, contention, and goroutine leaks.

3.1 Avoiding Goroutine Leaks

A **goroutine leak** occurs when goroutines are created but never terminated, causing memory and resource consumption to increase over time. Always ensure that goroutines exit when their work is done.

Here's an example of a potential goroutine leak:

119

```
func process(ch <-chan int) {
    for val := range ch {
        fmt.Println("Processing", val)
    }
}

func main() {
    ch := make(chan int)
    go process(ch)

    // If ch is never closed, the goroutine will leak
}
```

To avoid this, make sure to close channels or use a context to signal goroutines to exit:

```
func process(ctx context.Context, ch <-chan int) {
    for {
        select {
        case val := <-ch:
            fmt.Println("Processing", val)
        case <-ctx.Done():
            return  // Exit the goroutine when context is
            cancelled
        }
    }
}

func main() {
    ctx, cancel := context.WithCancel(context.Background())
    defer cancel()

    ch := make(chan int)
    go process(ctx, ch)

    // Cancel the context to stop the goroutine
    cancel()
}
```

3.2 Reducing Contention in Concurrent Code

Contention occurs when multiple goroutines compete for the same resource, such as a mutex. This can lead to performance bottlenecks.

- **Use Channels for Synchronization**: Instead of using mutexes, consider using channels to synchronize goroutines. Channels can provide better performance and simplify code by avoiding explicit locking and unlocking.

```go
ch := make(chan int)

go func() {
    ch <- 42   // Send value to the channel
}()

val := <-ch   // Receive value from the channel
fmt.Println(val)
```

- **Minimize Lock Granularity**: If you must use locks, try to minimize the critical section (the code protected by the lock) to reduce contention.

```go
mu.Lock()
// Only protect the critical part of the code
criticalData++
mu.Unlock()
```

3.3 Using Worker Pools

Worker pools, as discussed in Chapter 11, can help manage concurrency efficiently. Instead of creating a new goroutine for every task, you can limit the number of goroutines by using a pool of workers. This helps prevent excessive goroutine creation and reduces the overhead of managing them.

4. Optimizing I/O Operations

I/O operations, such as reading from files, making network requests, or writing to disk, are often the slowest parts of a program. Go provides several ways to optimize I/O for better performance.

4.1 Using Buffers for I/O

When reading or writing large amounts of data, using a buffer can significantly improve performance by reducing the number of system calls.

For example, when writing to a file:

```
file, _ := os.Create("output.txt")
defer file.Close()

writer := bufio.NewWriter(file)
for i := 0; i < 1000; i++ {
    writer.WriteString("Some data\n")
}
writer.Flush()  // Ensure all data is written to the file
```

Using a bufio.Writer reduces the number of write operations to the file, which is much more efficient than writing each line individually.

4.2 Asynchronous I/O with Goroutines

For I/O-bound tasks, you can use goroutines to perform asynchronous I/O operations without blocking the main thread. This allows your program to handle multiple I/O requests concurrently.

```
func fetchData(url string) {
    resp, err := http.Get(url)
    if err != nil {
        fmt.Println("Error fetching data:", err)
        return
    }
    defer resp.Body.Close()
    data, _ := ioutil.ReadAll(resp.Body)
    fmt.Println("Data fetched:", len(data), "bytes")
}

func main() {
    urls := []string{"https://example.com", "https://golang.org"}
```

```
    for _, url := range urls {
        go fetchData(url)
    }
    time.Sleep(2 * time.Second)   // Allow goroutines to finish
}
```

Here, each fetchData function runs in its own goroutine, allowing multiple HTTP requests to be processed concurrently.

5. Optimizing for Low Latency

In some applications, especially those that require real-time or low-latency responses, reducing response time is critical. Here are some strategies for optimizing Go applications for low latency:

- **Reduce GC Pressure**: Use techniques to minimize garbage collection, such as reducing allocations and using sync.Pool for object reuse.
- **Optimize Data Structures**: Choose the right data structures based on the operations you need. For example, using a map for fast lookups or a slice for efficient sequential access.
- **Profile Frequently**: Continuously profile your application using tools like pprof to identify performance bottlenecks and areas for optimization.
- **Use Context for Timeouts**: Ensure that goroutines do not block indefinitely by using the context package to enforce timeouts on operations like network requests or database queries.

Optimizing Go for performance involves understanding the trade-offs between memory usage, concurrency, and execution time. By using profiling tools like pprof, minimizing memory allocations, and leveraging Go's concurrency model efficiently, you can write Go programs that are not only correct but also highly performant.

In this chapter, we covered key techniques for optimizing Go applications, including profiling, memory management, concurrency optimization, and I/O performance. By applying these strategies, you'll be able to build scalable, fast, and efficient Go applications that can handle demanding workloads.

In the next chapter, we'll explore **working with Go's reflection and type system**, diving into how to manipulate and inspect types at runtime for more dynamic, flexible Go programs.

Deploying Go Applications

Once you've built your Go application, the next step is deployment—getting your application running efficiently in a production environment. Go is well-suited for deployment thanks to its static compilation, minimal runtime dependencies, and cross-platform capabilities. Whether you're deploying on bare-metal servers, virtual machines, containers, or cloud platforms, Go provides flexibility and performance.

In this chapter, we'll explore best practices for deploying Go applications, including compiling for different environments, containerization with Docker, setting up CI/CD pipelines, managing configuration, and scaling applications in production.

1. Compiling and Building Go Applications

One of Go's key advantages is its ability to compile applications into a single static binary, which makes deployment simple and portable.

1.1 Building a Binary for Your System

Building a binary for your local environment is straightforward. The go build command compiles your Go application into a binary that can be run on your system:

```
go build -o myapp
```

This generates an executable named myapp (or myapp.exe on Windows) in your current directory. The binary contains everything your application needs to run, including Go's runtime and any dependencies.

1.2 Cross-Compiling for Other Platforms

Go makes it easy to cross-compile binaries for different operating systems and architectures. This is especially useful if you're developing on one platform but need to deploy your application on another.

To cross-compile, set the GOOS (operating system) and GOARCH (architecture) environment variables before running go build.

For example, to compile for Linux on an AMD64 architecture:

```
GOOS=linux GOARCH=amd64 go build -o myapp-linux
```

To compile for Windows:

```
GOOS=windows GOARCH=amd64 go build -o myapp.exe
```

Go supports multiple target platforms, including Linux, Windows, macOS, FreeBSD, and others, making it highly flexible for deployment across different environments.

1.3 Static Binaries and Minimal Dependencies

Go produces static binaries by default, meaning they include all necessary libraries and do not require external dependencies at runtime. This makes your application highly portable, as it can run on any system without needing additional libraries or frameworks installed.

If you want to build a fully static binary (especially useful for Docker or Alpine Linux), you can pass the -ldflags option to strip unnecessary debugging information:

```
go build -ldflags="-s -w" -o myapp
```

This reduces the size of the binary, making it faster to deploy and distribute.

2. Environment Variables and Configuration Management

Managing configuration is a critical part of deploying applications, as it allows you to adjust settings such as database credentials, API keys, and service endpoints without hardcoding them into your application.

2.1 Using Environment Variables

Environment variables are a simple and effective way to manage configuration for Go applications. The os package provides functions to read environment variables in Go.

Here's an example of how to use environment variables to configure a Go application:

```
package main

import (
    "fmt"
    "os"
)

func main() {
    port := os.Getenv("APP_PORT")
    if port == "" {
        port = "8080"  // Default to 8080 if not set
    }
    fmt.Println("Running on port:", port)
}
```

In this example, the APP_PORT environment variable is used to specify the port the application should run on. If the variable is not set, the application defaults to port 8080.

When deploying, you can set environment variables using the command line or your orchestration tool (e.g., Docker, Kubernetes):

```
export APP_PORT=3000
./myapp
```

2.2 Using Configuration Files

While environment variables are great for simple configuration, more complex applications may require configuration files. You can store configuration in JSON, YAML, or TOML files and load them into your Go application.

Here's an example of loading configuration from a JSON file:

```go
import (
    "encoding/json"
    "fmt"
    "os"
)

type Config struct {
    Port    string `json:"port"`
    DBHost  string `json:"db_host"`
    DBUser  string `json:"db_user"`
    DBPass  string `json:"db_pass"`
}

func loadConfig(filename string) (*Config, error) {
    file, err := os.Open(filename)
    if err != nil {
        return nil, err
    }
    defer file.Close()

    config := &Config{}
    decoder := json.NewDecoder(file)
    if err := decoder.Decode(config); err != nil {
        return nil, err
    }

    return config, nil
}

func main() {
    config, err := loadConfig("config.json")
    if err != nil {
        fmt.Println("Error loading config:", err)
        return
    }
```

```
    fmt.Printf("Running on port %s with DB host %s\n",
    config.Port, config.DBHost)
}
```

In this example, the configuration is loaded from a config.json file at runtime. You can manage different configurations for development, testing, and production environments by using separate configuration files or environment variables to load different files dynamically.

3. Containerizing Go Applications with Docker

Docker is a popular tool for containerizing applications, making it easier to deploy, scale, and manage them across various environments. Since Go applications compile into static binaries, they are perfect for Docker deployment because they don't require a full OS or complex runtime dependencies.

3.1 Writing a Dockerfile for a Go Application

Here's an example of a minimal Dockerfile for a Go application:

```
# Step 1: Build the Go binary in a temporary container
FROM golang:1.18 as builder

WORKDIR /app

# Copy the Go source code
COPY . .

# Build the Go binary
RUN go build -o myapp .

# Step 2: Create a lightweight container for the application
FROM scratch

# Copy the binary from the builder stage
COPY --from=builder /app/myapp /myapp

# Expose the port and run the binary
```

```
EXPOSE 8080
ENTRYPOINT ["/myapp"]
```

This Dockerfile follows a multi-stage build pattern:

- The **builder stage** uses the official Go image to compile the application.
- The final image uses **scratch**, which is an empty, minimal base image, making the resulting image very small (often under 10 MB).

To build the Docker image:

```
docker build -t myapp .
```

To run the container:

```
docker run -p 8080:8080 myapp
```

This exposes the application on port 8080 inside the container and maps it to port 8080 on your local machine.

3.2 Using Alpine Linux for Smaller Images

If you want a slightly more flexible image (e.g., for debugging), you can use Alpine Linux, a lightweight distribution. This results in a slightly larger image but offers more utilities.

Here's an example Dockerfile using Alpine:

```
FROM golang:1.18-alpine as builder

WORKDIR /app
COPY . .
RUN go build -o myapp .

FROM alpine

RUN apk add --no-cache ca-certificates
```

```
COPY --from=builder /app/myapp /myapp

EXPOSE 8080
ENTRYPOINT ["/myapp"]
```

Alpine-based images are small and efficient while still giving you access to a Linux environment.

4. Continuous Integration and Continuous Deployment (CI/CD)

CI/CD pipelines automate the process of building, testing, and deploying your Go application, ensuring that code changes are integrated regularly and deployed seamlessly. There are many CI/CD tools available, such as **GitHub Actions, GitLab CI, Jenkins**, and **CircleCI**.

4.1 Setting Up a CI Pipeline with GitHub Actions

Here's an example of a basic CI pipeline using GitHub Actions to build and test a Go application:

1. Create a .github/workflows/go.yml file in your repository:

```
name: Go CI

on:
  push:
    branches:
      - main

jobs:
  build:
    runs-on: ubuntu-latest

    steps:
      - name: Checkout code
        uses: actions/checkout@v2
```

```
  - name: Set up Go
    uses: actions/setup-go@v2
    with:
      go-version: 1.18

  - name: Build
    run: go build -v ./...

  - name: Run tests
    run: go test -v ./...
```

This pipeline runs on every push to the main branch and:

- Checks out the code from the repository.
- Sets up Go 1.18.
- Builds the application.
- Runs tests to ensure code quality.

4.2 Deploying with CI/CD

You can integrate deployment into your CI/CD pipeline. For example, you could use GitHub Actions to build and push a Docker image to a container registry like Docker Hub, then trigger a deployment to Kubernetes, AWS, or Google Cloud.

Here's how you might build and push a Docker image using GitHub Actions:

```
jobs:
  build-and-deploy:
    runs-on: ubuntu-latest

    steps:
      - name: Checkout code
        uses: actions/checkout@v2

      - name: Build Docker image
```

```
    run: docker build -t myapp .

  - name: Log in to Docker Hub
    run: echo "${{ secrets.DOCKER_PASSWORD }}" | docker login
    -u "${{ secrets.DOCKER_USERNAME }}" --password-stdin

  - name: Push Docker image
    run: docker push myapp
```

In this example, the Docker image is built and pushed to Docker Hub, and you can add further steps to deploy it to your preferred hosting platform.

5. Scaling Go Applications

Once your Go application is deployed, you may need to scale it to handle more traffic or distribute the load across multiple instances. There are several strategies for scaling Go applications.

5.1 Horizontal Scaling with Load Balancers

One common approach to scaling web applications is **horizontal scaling**, where multiple instances of the application run concurrently behind a load balancer. A load balancer distributes incoming requests across the available instances, improving throughput and reliability.

Many cloud providers, such as AWS (with **Elastic Load Balancing**) and Google Cloud (with **Google Cloud Load Balancer**), offer built-in load balancing services. You can also use third-party tools like **Nginx** or **HAProxy**.

5.2 Auto-scaling with Containers

Using containers, you can easily scale Go applications by deploying them in container orchestration platforms like **Kubernetes** or **Docker Swarm**. These platforms support auto-scaling, allowing the number of running instances to increase or decrease based on CPU usage, memory consumption, or request volume.

For example, in Kubernetes, you can set up **Horizontal Pod Autoscaling (HPA)** to automatically scale the number of pods running your Go application:

```
apiVersion: autoscaling/v1
kind: HorizontalPodAutoscaler
metadata:
  name: myapp-hpa
spec:
  scaleTargetRef:
    apiVersion: apps/v1
    kind: Deployment
    name: myapp
  minReplicas: 2
  maxReplicas: 10
  targetCPUUtilizationPercentage: 80
```

In this example, Kubernetes automatically scales the deployment of your Go application based on CPU utilization, ensuring that it can handle increased traffic while conserving resources during low traffic periods.

5.3 Monitoring and Logging

Effective monitoring and logging are essential to understand the health and performance of your Go application in production. You can use tools like **Prometheus** for metrics collection and **Grafana** for visualization. For logging, consider **ELK stack** (Elasticsearch, Logstash, Kibana) or managed services like **Datadog** or **Loggly**.

You can instrument your Go application with metrics using the **Prometheus client library**:

```
import (
    "github.com/prometheus/client_golang/prometheus"
    "github.com/prometheus/client_golang/prometheus/promhttp"
    "net/http"
)

var requestCount = prometheus.NewCounterVec(
    prometheus.CounterOpts{
        Name: "http_requests_total",
        Help: "Number of HTTP requests processed",
```

```
    },
    []string{"method", "status"},
)

func init() {
    prometheus.MustRegister(requestCount)
}

func handler(w http.ResponseWriter, r *http.Request) {
    requestCount.WithLabelValues(r.Method, "200").Inc()
    w.Write([]byte("Hello, world!"))
}

func main() {
    http.Handle("/metrics", promhttp.Handler())
    http.HandleFunc("/", handler)
    http.ListenAndServe(":8080", nil)
}
```

This code exposes metrics on the /metrics endpoint, which Prometheus can scrape to gather statistics about your application.

In this chapter, we explored how to deploy Go applications, covering everything from building static binaries to containerizing your application with Docker, managing configuration through environment variables, and setting up CI/CD pipelines. We also discussed scaling strategies, including horizontal scaling with load balancers, auto-scaling with Kubernetes, and monitoring for production environments.

With Go's efficient compilation process, containerization capabilities, and support for modern CI/CD and cloud platforms, deploying Go applications is simple and scalable, enabling you to build robust, high-performance systems that can grow with your needs.

In the next chapter, we'll dive into **working with Go's reflection and type system**, where we'll explore dynamic type manipulation and how to write flexible code that can adapt to different types at runtime.

Go in the Cloud and Microservices

The rise of cloud computing and microservices architectures has transformed how modern applications are developed and deployed. Go's speed, simplicity, and efficient memory usage make it an excellent choice for building cloud-native applications and microservices. Whether you're deploying a single service or scaling a complex distributed system, Go provides the tools and ecosystem to handle cloud environments with ease.

In this chapter, we'll explore how to design, develop, and deploy Go applications in the cloud, leveraging cloud platforms, building microservices, using cloud-native patterns, and managing communication between services. We'll also look at best practices for monitoring, scaling, and securing Go microservices in a cloud environment.

1. Why Go is Ideal for Cloud and Microservices

Go was designed to handle the challenges of building scalable and distributed systems. Several key features make Go ideal for cloud-native applications and microservices:

- **Concurrency**: Go's lightweight goroutines and channels enable it to handle high levels of concurrency efficiently, making it perfect for microservices that need to handle many requests simultaneously.
- **Simplicity**: Go's clean syntax and minimal design reduce complexity in building services that are easy to maintain, deploy, and scale.
- **Performance**: Go compiles to fast, statically linked binaries with mini-

mal overhead, making it an excellent choice for resource-constrained cloud environments.

- **Small Memory Footprint**: Go's efficient memory usage and garbage collector are optimized for building high-performance applications that run in containers and cloud environments.
- **Fast Compilation**: Go's fast compilation times make it suitable for rapid development cycles, continuous integration, and deployment pipelines.

2. Building Microservices in Go

Microservices are an architectural style where an application is composed of multiple, independent services that communicate over the network. Each service handles a specific domain or business functionality, and microservices are typically deployed in containers and scaled independently.

2.1 Structuring a Microservice

A Go microservice is typically structured around the following components:

- **HTTP Handlers**: Handle incoming requests (e.g., RESTful API requests).
- **Business Logic**: The core functionality of the service.
- **Data Layer**: Manages data access (e.g., databases, external APIs).
- **Communication Layer**: Manages communication with other services (e.g., gRPC or REST calls).
- **Middleware**: Adds common functionality such as logging, authentication, or rate limiting.

Here's an example of a simple Go microservice that handles user management:

```
package main

import (
    "encoding/json"
    "net/http"
```

```
    "log"
)

type User struct {
    ID    int    `json:"id"`
    Name string `json:"name"`
}

var users = []User{
    {ID: 1, Name: "Alice"},
    {ID: 2, Name: "Bob"},
}

func getUsers(w http.ResponseWriter, r *http.Request) {
    w.Header().Set("Content-Type", "application/json")
    json.NewEncoder(w).Encode(users)
}

func main() {
    http.HandleFunc("/users", getUsers)
    log.Println("Starting server on :8080")
    log.Fatal(http.ListenAndServe(":8080", nil))
}
```

In this basic example:

- We define a simple HTTP handler (getUsers) to serve a list of users.
- The main function starts the HTTP server on port 8080.

This is a basic foundation of a microservice that can be extended with database access, external API calls, or more complex business logic.

2.2 Communication Between Microservices

Microservices typically communicate over HTTP or gRPC. Go provides strong support for both approaches, and each has its advantages.

- **RESTful HTTP**: This is a common pattern where services expose endpoints that respond with JSON over HTTP. It's simple to implement using Go's net/http package or frameworks like **Gin** or **Echo**.

- Example of making an HTTP request between microservices:

```
resp, err := http.Get("http://service-b:8080/api/resource")
if err != nil {
    log.Fatal(err)
}
defer resp.Body.Close()
```

- **gRPC**: gRPC is a high-performance RPC (Remote Procedure Call) framework developed by Google. It uses Protocol Buffers (protobuf) for efficient serialization and supports features like streaming and bi-directional communication. Go has excellent support for gRPC, making it ideal for high-performance microservices.
- Here's how to define a gRPC service in Go:

1. Define the service in a .proto file:

```
syntax = "proto3";

service UserService {
  rpc GetUser (UserRequest) returns (UserResponse);
}

message UserRequest {
  int32 id = 1;
}

message UserResponse {
  int32 id = 1;
  string name = 2;
}
```

1. Generate the Go code using the protoc compiler and protoc-gen-go.
2. Implement the service in Go:

```
type server struct{}

func (s *server) GetUser(ctx context.Context, req
*pb.UserRequest) (*pb.UserResponse, error) {
    user := &pb.UserResponse{
        Id:   req.Id,
        Name: "Alice",
    }
    return user, nil
}
```

1. Start the gRPC server:

```
lis, err := net.Listen("tcp", ":50051")
if err != nil {
    log.Fatalf("Failed to listen: %v", err)
}
s := grpc.NewServer()
pb.RegisterUserServiceServer(s, &server{})
log.Println("gRPC server running on port 50051")
if err := s.Serve(lis); err != nil {
    log.Fatalf("Failed to serve: %v", err)
}
```

2.3 Using Middleware in Microservices

Middleware in microservices adds layers of functionality, such as logging, error handling, or rate limiting. Middleware can be implemented using the http.Handler interface or middleware frameworks like **Gin** or **Echo**.

Here's an example of a simple logging middleware in Go:

```go
func loggingMiddleware(next http.Handler) http.Handler {
    return http.HandlerFunc(func(w http.ResponseWriter, r
    *http.Request) {
        log.Printf("Request: %s %s", r.Method, r.URL.Path)
        next.ServeHTTP(w, r)
    })
}

func main() {
    mux := http.NewServeMux()
    mux.HandleFunc("/users", getUsers)

    wrappedMux := loggingMiddleware(mux)
    log.Println("Starting server on :8080")
    log.Fatal(http.ListenAndServe(":8080", wrappedMux))
}
```

In this example, the loggingMiddleware function wraps the HTTP handler and logs every request before passing control to the next handler.

3. Deploying Go Microservices in the Cloud

Once your Go microservice is ready, deploying it to the cloud requires setting up containers, managing orchestration, and ensuring proper networking and scaling.

3.1 Containerizing Microservices with Docker

As with any Go application, microservices can be containerized using Docker. A typical Dockerfile for a Go microservice looks like this:

```dockerfile
FROM golang:1.18 as builder

WORKDIR /app
COPY . .

# Build the Go binary
RUN go build -o myservice .

# Create a minimal image with just the binary
```

```
FROM alpine
COPY --from=builder /app/myservice /myservice
EXPOSE 8080
ENTRYPOINT ["/myservice"]
```

After building the Docker image:

```
docker build -t myservice .
docker run -p 8080:8080 myservice
```

You can deploy the Docker container to any cloud service, such as AWS, Google Cloud, or Azure, or use a container orchestration platform like **Kubernetes** for more complex deployments.

3.2 Deploying to Kubernetes

Kubernetes is a powerful orchestration tool for managing containers in the cloud. It handles scheduling, scaling, load balancing, and fault tolerance.

Here's a basic Kubernetes deployment for a Go microservice:

1. Create a Kubernetes **Deployment** and **Service** YAML file:

```
apiVersion: apps/v1
kind: Deployment
metadata:
  name: myservice-deployment
spec:
  replicas: 3
  selector:
    matchLabels:
      app: myservice
  template:
    metadata:
      labels:
        app: myservice
    spec:
```

```
containers:
- name: myservice
  image: myservice:latest
  ports:
  - containerPort: 8080


---

apiVersion: v1
kind: Service
metadata:
  name: myservice
spec:
  selector:
    app: myservice
  ports:
    - protocol: TCP
      port: 80
      targetPort: 8080
  type: LoadBalancer
```

1. Deploy to Kubernetes:

```
kubectl apply -f myservice.yaml
```

This creates a Kubernetes deployment with three replicas of your Go microservice and exposes it via a load balancer.

3.3 Scaling Go Microservices in Kubernetes

Kubernetes makes it easy to scale Go microservices horizontally by adjusting the number of replicas. You can use the kubectl scale command to scale your service:

```
kubectl scale deployment myservice-deployment --replicas=5
```

Kubernetes also supports **Horizontal Pod Autoscaling (HPA)**, which allows your service to scale automatically based on CPU or memory usage:

```
apiVersion: autoscaling/v1
kind: HorizontalPodAutoscaler
metadata:
  name: myservice-hpa
spec:
  scaleTargetRef:
    apiVersion: apps/v1
    kind: Deployment
    name: myservice-deployment
  minReplicas: 2
  maxReplicas: 10
  targetCPUUtilizationPercentage: 80
```

This automatically scales the service up or down based on CPU usage.

4. Cloud-Native Go Patterns

When deploying Go microservices in the cloud, there are several patterns and practices to ensure that your application is scalable, fault-tolerant, and maintainable.

4.1 Circuit Breaker Pattern

The **circuit breaker** pattern is a fault-tolerance technique that prevents your microservice from making requests to a failing service, helping to avoid cascading failures.

There are libraries like **go-resiliency** that can help implement the circuit breaker pattern in Go.

```
import (
    "github.com/eapache/go-resiliency/breaker"
    "net/http"
    "log"
)

func main() {
```

```go
br := breaker.New(3, 1, 5*time.Second)

result := br.Run(func() error {
    resp, err := http.Get("http://unreliable-service/api")
    if err != nil {
        return err
    }
    defer resp.Body.Close()
    return nil
})

if result == breaker.ErrBreakerOpen {
    log.Println("Circuit breaker open, skipping request")
} else if result != nil {
    log.Println("Request failed:", result)
} else {
    log.Println("Request succeeded")
}
}
```

4.2 API Gateway

In a microservices architecture, it's common to use an **API Gateway** as a single entry point for all microservices. The API Gateway handles routing, authentication, and load balancing, simplifying the architecture and improving security.

Tools like **Kong, NGINX,** or **Envoy** are popular API gateways that can be deployed alongside Go microservices.

5. Monitoring, Logging, and Observability

Cloud environments require robust monitoring and logging to track service performance and identify issues. Go applications can easily integrate with monitoring tools like **Prometheus** and logging frameworks like **Logrus** or **Zap**.

5.1 Metrics with Prometheus

You can export metrics from Go applications using the **Prometheus** client library. Here's how to instrument a Go microservice for Prometheus:

```go
import (
    "github.com/prometheus/client_golang/prometheus"
    "github.com/prometheus/client_golang/prometheus/promhttp"
    "net/http"
)

var requestCount = prometheus.NewCounterVec(
    prometheus.CounterOpts{
        Name: "http_requests_total",
        Help: "Total number of HTTP requests",
    },
    []string{"method", "status"},
)

func init() {
    prometheus.MustRegister(requestCount)
}

func handler(w http.ResponseWriter, r *http.Request) {
    requestCount.WithLabelValues(r.Method, "200").Inc()
    w.Write([]byte("Hello, World!"))
}

func main() {
    http.Handle("/metrics", promhttp.Handler()) // Prometheus
    metrics endpoint
    http.HandleFunc("/", handler)
    http.ListenAndServe(":8080", nil)
}
```

Prometheus can scrape the /metrics endpoint to collect statistics about the service's performance.

5.2 Distributed Tracing

For microservices, distributed tracing is crucial for tracking requests as they flow through multiple services. **OpenTelemetry** is an emerging standard for distributed tracing and is well-supported in Go.

You can instrument your Go application for tracing with OpenTelemetry:

```
go get go.opentelemetry.io/otel
```

With tracing, you can identify latency issues, bottlenecks, and failures across the microservice architecture.

In this chapter, we explored how to build, deploy, and manage Go microservices in cloud environments. From structuring microservices and managing inter-service communication to deploying containers with Docker and Kubernetes, Go offers a powerful and flexible foundation for cloud-native development. We also covered essential cloud-native patterns such as the circuit breaker, API gateways, and monitoring techniques that ensure your services remain scalable, resilient, and observable.

By applying these practices, you can leverage Go to build robust microservice architectures that can scale with your needs, handle cloud deployments efficiently, and ensure the best performance for your applications.

In the next chapter, we'll dive into **working with Go's reflection and type system**, exploring how Go allows you to manipulate types at runtime and build more flexible, dynamic applications.

Handling Files and Working with APIs

I n many applications, handling files and interacting with external APIs are common tasks. Whether you're processing file uploads, reading configuration files, or fetching data from a REST API, Go provides robust support for both file handling and API consumption. This chapter will guide you through handling files in Go and interacting with external APIs, focusing on best practices, common patterns, and practical examples.

We will cover:

- Reading and writing files in Go
- Handling file uploads in web applications
- Working with JSON and XML formats
- Interacting with REST APIs
- Error handling and retries in API requests

1. Handling Files in Go

Go's standard library provides extensive support for working with files, including reading, writing, creating, and managing file permissions. The os, io, and bufio packages contain most of the functions you'll need to manipulate files in Go.

1.1 Reading Files

To read a file in Go, you can use the os.Open function, which returns a file descriptor. Once you have the file descriptor, you can read the contents using functions like Read, ReadAll, or use the bufio package for buffered reading.

Here's a simple example of reading a file and printing its contents:

```go
package main

import (
    "fmt"
    "io/ioutil"
    "log"
    "os"
)

func main() {
    file, err := os.Open("example.txt")
    if err != nil {
        log.Fatal(err)
    }
    defer file.Close()

    content, err := ioutil.ReadAll(file)  // Read the file content
    if err != nil {
        log.Fatal(err)
    }

    fmt.Println(string(content))
}
```

In this example:

- We open a file named example.txt using os.Open.
- The ioutil.ReadAll function reads the entire file content into memory, and we print it as a string.

If the file is large, it's more efficient to read it in chunks using a buffered reader:

```go
package main
```

```
import (
    "bufio"
    "fmt"
    "log"
    "os"
)

func main() {
    file, err := os.Open("example.txt")
    if err != nil {
        log.Fatal(err)
    }
    defer file.Close()

    scanner := bufio.NewScanner(file)
    for scanner.Scan() {
        fmt.Println(scanner.Text())  // Print each line
    }

    if err := scanner.Err(); err != nil {
        log.Fatal(err)
    }
}
```

This code reads the file line-by-line using a buffered scanner, which is more memory-efficient for large files.

1.2 Writing Files

Writing to files in Go is straightforward using the os.Create or os.OpenFile functions, which create or open a file for writing. You can then use the Write or WriteString methods to write data to the file.

Here's an example of creating and writing to a file:

```
package main

import (
    "fmt"
    "os"
```

```
)

func main() {
    file, err := os.Create("output.txt")
    if err != nil {
        fmt.Println("Error creating file:", err)
        return
    }
    defer file.Close()

    file.WriteString("Hello, Go!\n")
    fmt.Println("File written successfully")
}
```

In this example, we create a new file called output.txt and write a string to it using WriteString.

1.3 File Operations: Copying, Moving, and Deleting

You can perform file operations like copying, moving, and deleting using Go's built-in functions.

- **Copying Files**: Use the io.Copy function to copy data from one file to another:

```
package main

import (
    "io"
    "os"
)

func main() {
    srcFile, err := os.Open("source.txt")
    if err != nil {
        panic(err)
    }
    defer srcFile.Close()
```

```
    dstFile, err := os.Create("destination.txt")
    if err != nil {
        panic(err)
    }
    defer dstFile.Close()

    _, err = io.Copy(dstFile, srcFile)   // Copy the contents
    if err != nil {
        panic(err)
    }

    println("File copied successfully")
}
```

- **Renaming or Moving Files**: Use os.Rename to move or rename a file:

```
err := os.Rename("old.txt", "new.txt")
if err != nil {
    fmt.Println("Error renaming file:", err)
}
```

- **Deleting Files**: Use os.Remove to delete a file:

```
err := os.Remove("file.txt")
if err != nil {
    fmt.Println("Error deleting file:", err)
}
```

2. Handling File Uploads in Web Applications

Handling file uploads is a common requirement in web applications. Go's net/http package provides built-in support for handling file uploads in HTTP requests.

2.1 Processing File Uploads

Here's an example of a basic file upload handler in Go:

```go
package main

import (
    "fmt"
    "io"
    "net/http"
    "os"
)

func uploadFile(w http.ResponseWriter, r *http.Request) {
    if r.Method != "POST" {
        http.Error(w, "Invalid request method",
        http.StatusMethodNotAllowed)
        return
    }

    file, handler, err := r.FormFile("uploadfile")
    if err != nil {
        http.Error(w, err.Error(), http.StatusInternalServerError)
        return
    }
    defer file.Close()

    outFile, err := os.Create(handler.Filename)
    if err != nil {
        http.Error(w, err.Error(), http.StatusInternalServerError)
        return
    }
    defer outFile.Close()

    _, err = io.Copy(outFile, file)  // Copy the uploaded file to
    the server
    if err != nil {
        http.Error(w, err.Error(), http.StatusInternalServerError)
        return
    }
```

```
    fmt.Fprintf(w, "File uploaded successfully: %s\n",
    handler.Filename)
}

func main() {
    http.HandleFunc("/upload", uploadFile)
    fmt.Println("Server started at :8080")
    http.ListenAndServe(":8080", nil)
}
```

In this example:

- The uploadFile function handles file uploads via HTTP POST requests.
- The r.FormFile function retrieves the uploaded file from the form, and io.Copy writes it to the server.

To upload a file, you would typically submit an HTML form like this:

```
<form enctype="multipart/form-data" action="/upload"
method="post">
    <input type="file" name="uploadfile" />
    <input type="submit" value="Upload File" />
</form>
```

3. Working with JSON and XML Formats

Working with structured data formats like JSON and XML is essential for both file handling and API communication. Go has excellent support for encoding and decoding JSON and XML using the encoding/json and encoding/xml packages.

3.1 JSON Encoding and Decoding

JSON is the most commonly used data format for web applications and APIs. Go makes it easy to marshal (encode) and unmarshal (decode) JSON.

Here's an example of encoding Go structs into JSON:

```go
package main

import (
    "encoding/json"
    "fmt"
)

type User struct {
    ID   int    `json:"id"`
    Name string `json:"name"`
}

func main() {
    user := User{ID: 1, Name: "Alice"}

    jsonData, err := json.Marshal(user)
    if err != nil {
        fmt.Println("Error encoding JSON:", err)
        return
    }

    fmt.Println(string(jsonData))
}
```

To decode JSON data into Go structs:

```go
package main

import (
    "encoding/json"
    "fmt"
)

type User struct {
    ID   int    `json:"id"`
    Name string `json:"name"`
}

func main() {
```

```
jsonString := `{"id": 1, "name": "Alice"}`

var user User
err := json.Unmarshal([]byte(jsonString), &user)
if err != nil {
    fmt.Println("Error decoding JSON:", err)
    return
}

fmt.Printf("ID: %d, Name: %s\n", user.ID, user.Name)
}
```

3.2 XML Encoding and Decoding

While JSON is more common, XML is still used in various applications. Go's encoding/xml package provides similar functionality for XML.

Here's an example of encoding and decoding XML in Go:

```
package main

import (
    "encoding/xml"
    "fmt"
)

type User struct {
    ID    int    `xml:"id"`
    Name string `xml:"name"`
}

func main() {
    user := User{ID: 1, Name: "Alice"}

    xmlData, err := xml.Marshal(user)
    if err != nil {
        fmt.Println("Error encoding XML:", err)
        return
    }
```

```
fmt.Println(string(xmlData))

// Decoding XML
xmlString := `<User><id>1</id><name>Alice</name></User>`
var decodedUser User
err = xml.Unmarshal([]byte(xmlString), &decodedUser)
if err != nil {
    fmt.Println("Error decoding XML:", err)
    return
}

fmt.Printf("ID: %d, Name: %s\n", decodedUser.ID,
decodedUser.Name)
}
```

4. Interacting with REST APIs

Go's net/http package is well-suited for interacting with REST APIs. Whether you're making GET requests, sending data with POST requests, or handling API errors, Go provides the tools you need for effective API communication.

4.1 Making GET Requests

To fetch data from a REST API, use the http.Get function:

```
package main

import (
    "fmt"
    "io/ioutil"
    "net/http"
)

func main() {
    resp, err :=
    http.Get("https://jsonplaceholder.typicode.com/posts/1")
    if err != nil {
        fmt.Println("Error making request:", err)
        return
```

```
    }
    defer resp.Body.Close()

    body, err := ioutil.ReadAll(resp.Body)
    if err != nil {
        fmt.Println("Error reading response:", err)
        return
    }

    fmt.Println(string(body))
}
```

In this example, we make a GET request to a sample API and print the response body.

4.2 Sending POST Requests with JSON Data

To send data to an API, you can use the http.Post or http.NewRequest functions.

Here's an example of sending a POST request with JSON data:

```
package main

import (
    "bytes"
    "encoding/json"
    "fmt"
    "net/http"
)

type Post struct {
    Title  string `json:"title"`
    Body   string `json:"body"`
    UserID int    `json:"userId"`
}

func main() {
    post := Post{
        Title: "Hello, Go!",
        Body:  "This is a post about Go.",
```

```
        UserID: 1,
    }

    jsonData, err := json.Marshal(post)
    if err != nil {
        fmt.Println("Error encoding JSON:", err)
        return
    }

    resp, err :=
    http.Post("https://jsonplaceholder.typicode.com/posts",
    "application/json", bytes.NewBuffer(jsonData))
    if err != nil {
        fmt.Println("Error making POST request:", err)
        return
    }
    defer resp.Body.Close()

    fmt.Println("Post request sent successfully!")
}
```

In this example:

- We marshal a Post struct into JSON.
- We send the JSON data in a POST request to a REST API using http.Post.

4.3 Handling API Errors and Retries

When interacting with APIs, it's important to handle errors and retry failed requests gracefully.

Here's an example that handles errors and retries on failure:

```
package main

import (
    "fmt"
    "net/http"
    "time"
```

```
)

func fetchData(url string) (*http.Response, error) {
    client := &http.Client{}
    for retries := 0; retries < 3; retries++ {
        resp, err := client.Get(url)
        if err != nil || resp.StatusCode != http.StatusOK {
            fmt.Println("Error fetching data, retrying...")
            time.Sleep(2 * time.Second)
            continue
        }
        return resp, nil
    }
    return nil, fmt.Errorf("failed to fetch data after 3
    attempts")
}

func main() {
    resp, err :=
    fetchData("https://jsonplaceholder.typicode.com/posts/1")
    if err != nil {
        fmt.Println("Error:", err)
        return
    }
    defer resp.Body.Close()

    fmt.Println("Data fetched successfully!")
}
```

In this example:

- We implement a retry mechanism that attempts to fetch data up to three times if there's an error or the response status code is not 200 OK.

In this chapter, we covered handling files in Go, from reading and writing files to handling file uploads in web applications. We also explored working with structured data formats such as JSON and XML and interacting with

REST APIs, including making GET and POST requests, handling errors, and implementing retries.

These skills are essential for many real-world applications, where file processing and API communication are critical components. By mastering these techniques, you'll be well-equipped to build robust, file-driven, and API-integrated Go applications.

In the next chapter, we will dive into **working with Go's reflection and type system**, where we'll explore dynamic type manipulation and writing flexible code that can adapt to different types at runtime.

Debugging and Error Handling in Production

Effective debugging and error handling are crucial for running reliable and robust Go applications in production. Errors in production systems can lead to unexpected failures, data loss, and poor user experience. Go provides built-in mechanisms for error handling, and with the right tools and techniques, you can trace issues, debug efficiently, and manage errors in a way that ensures system stability.

In this chapter, we will explore best practices for error handling, techniques for debugging Go applications in production, and tools for monitoring, logging, and diagnosing issues.

1. Error Handling in Go

Error handling is an essential part of Go programming. Unlike many other languages that rely on exceptions, Go uses explicit error handling through return values. This approach promotes cleaner, more predictable code by making error cases part of the function's signature.

1.1 Returning and Checking Errors

In Go, errors are handled explicitly by returning an error type from a function. A common pattern is to check for errors immediately after a function call and handle them accordingly.

Here's an example of basic error handling:

```go
package main

import (
    "errors"
    "fmt"
)

func divide(a, b int) (int, error) {
    if b == 0 {
        return 0, errors.New("cannot divide by zero")
    }
    return a / b, nil
}

func main() {
    result, err := divide(4, 0)
    if err != nil {
        fmt.Println("Error:", err)
        return
    }
    fmt.Println("Result:", result)
}
```

In this example, we return an error when trying to divide by zero. The calling function checks if the error is non-nil and handles it accordingly.

1.2 Using Custom Error Types

In addition to basic error handling, Go allows you to create custom error types by implementing the error interface. This can be useful for providing more detailed error information.

Here's an example of a custom error type:

```go
package main

import (
    "fmt"
)
```

```go
type DivideError struct {
    Dividend int
    Divisor  int
}

func (e *DivideError) Error() string {
    return fmt.Sprintf("cannot divide %d by %d", e.Dividend,
    e.Divisor)
}

func divide(a, b int) (int, error) {
    if b == 0 {
        return 0, &DivideError{Dividend: a, Divisor: b}
    }
    return a / b, nil
}

func main() {
    result, err := divide(4, 0)
    if err != nil {
        fmt.Println("Error:", err)
        return
    }
    fmt.Println("Result:", result)
}
```

This approach makes it easier to inspect and differentiate between various error types in your code, which is particularly helpful in production systems where you need detailed error information for logging and monitoring.

2. Error Wrapping and Stack Traces

Go 1.13 introduced **error wrapping**, which allows you to wrap errors to retain context as they propagate through the program. This helps trace the origin of errors and adds context that is useful for debugging.

2.1 Wrapping Errors with fmt.Errorf

You can wrap errors using fmt.Errorf with the %w verb, which allows errors to retain their original context while adding additional information.

```
package main

import (
    "errors"
    "fmt"
    "os"
)

func readFile(filename string) error {
    _, err := os.Open(filename)
    if err != nil {
        return fmt.Errorf("failed to open file %s: %w", filename,
        err)
    }
    return nil
}

func main() {
    err := readFile("nonexistent.txt")
    if err != nil {
        fmt.Println("Error:", err)
    }
}
```

In this example, the error message retains the original os.Open error but adds context with the filename, making it easier to understand what went wrong.

2.2 Unwrapping Errors

To check for specific error types in a wrapped error, you can use the errors.Is and errors.As functions:

- **errors.Is** checks if an error matches a target error.
- **errors.As** checks if an error can be cast to a specific error type.

```go
package main

import (
    "errors"
    "fmt"
    "os"
)

func readFile(filename string) error {
    _, err := os.Open(filename)
    if err != nil {
        return fmt.Errorf("failed to open file %s: %w", filename,
        err)
    }
    return nil
}

func main() {
    err := readFile("nonexistent.txt")
    if errors.Is(err, os.ErrNotExist) {
        fmt.Println("File does not exist:", err)
    }
}
```

This technique allows you to identify specific errors even if they are wrapped, improving the clarity and handling of errors in production.

3. Debugging in Production

Debugging in production environments can be challenging, as it often involves identifying issues without stopping the service or having direct access to the development environment. Go provides several tools and techniques to debug applications running in production.

3.1 Using Logs for Debugging

Logs are the most common way to gain insight into a running application. Structured logging provides context and detail, helping you trace the execution flow and identify potential issues.

Go's standard log package provides basic logging functionality, but you can use third-party logging libraries like **Logrus** or **Zap** for more advanced features such as structured logs, log levels, and performance optimization.

Here's an example using the log package:

```
package main

import (
    "log"
    "os"
)

func main() {
    file, err := os.Open("example.txt")
    if err != nil {
        log.Fatalf("Error opening file: %v", err)
    }
    defer file.Close()

    log.Println("File opened successfully")
}
```

For more sophisticated logging, **Logrus** provides a structured logging interface:

```
package main

import (
    log "github.com/sirupsen/logrus"
    "os"
)

func main() {
    file, err := os.Open("example.txt")
    if err != nil {
        log.WithFields(log.Fields{
            "filename": "example.txt",
        }).Fatal("Error opening file")
    }
```

```
    defer file.Close()

    log.Info("File opened successfully")
}
```

3.2 Using Panic and Recover

Although Go discourages the use of panics for normal error handling, panics are useful for catching unexpected, critical issues that indicate a program bug. In production systems, you can use recover to gracefully handle panics and prevent application crashes.

Here's how to use panic and recover in a Go application:

```
package main

import (
    "fmt"
)

func safeDivide(a, b int) {
    defer func() {
        if r := recover(); r != nil {
            fmt.Println("Recovered from panic:", r)
        }
    }()
    fmt.Println(a / b)
}

func main() {
    safeDivide(4, 0)
    fmt.Println("Program continues after panic recovery")
}
```

In this example, the panic caused by dividing by zero is caught by recover, allowing the program to continue running without crashing.

3.3 Profiling and Tracing with pprof

Go's pprof package provides built-in tools for profiling CPU, memory, and goroutines. Profiling is an essential technique for understanding performance bottlenecks, memory usage, and identifying slow-running code in production systems.

Here's how to enable profiling in a Go web application:

```
package main

import (
    "log"
    "net/http"
    _ "net/http/pprof"
)

func main() {
    go func() {
        log.Println(http.ListenAndServe("localhost:6060", nil))
        // Starts pprof server
    }()

    log.Println("Application running...")
    select {} // Keeps the application running
}
```

After enabling pprof, you can access profiling data at http://localhost:6060/debug/pprof/. You can then use go tool pprof to analyze the performance data:

```
go tool pprof http://localhost:6060/debug/pprof/profile
```

This will open an interactive profiling tool that helps you identify performance bottlenecks and memory issues.

4. Monitoring and Observability

In production, continuous monitoring and observability are crucial to identifying and fixing issues before they impact users. With tools like **Prometheus** and **Grafana** for metrics, and **OpenTelemetry** for tracing, you can gain deep insights into your Go applications in real time.

4.1 Metrics with Prometheus

You can instrument your Go application to expose custom metrics for Prometheus. For example, here's how to track HTTP request counts and response times:

```go
package main

import (
    "github.com/prometheus/client_golang/prometheus"
    "github.com/prometheus/client_golang/prometheus/promhttp"
    "net/http"
)

var requestCount = prometheus.NewCounterVec(
    prometheus.CounterOpts{
        Name: "http_requests_total",
        Help: "Total number of HTTP requests",
    },
    []string{"path", "status"},
)

func init() {
    prometheus.MustRegister(requestCount)
}

func handler(w http.ResponseWriter, r *http.Request) {
    requestCount.WithLabelValues(r.URL.Path, "200").Inc()
    w.Write([]byte("Hello, world!"))
}

func main() {
    http.Handle("/metrics", promhttp.Handler())
    http.HandleFunc("/", handler)
    http.ListenAndServe(":8080", nil)
}
```

Prometheus can scrape the /metrics endpoint to collect metrics data, and you can visualize these metrics in **Grafana** to monitor system performance in real-time.

4.2 Distributed Tracing with OpenTelemetry

OpenTelemetry provides a standard for distributed tracing, enabling you to trace requests across multiple services. This is particularly useful in microservices architectures.

Here's a basic example of using OpenTelemetry in a Go application:

```go
package main

import (
    "context"
    "fmt"
    "go.opentelemetry.io/otel"
    "go.opentelemetry.io/otel/trace"
)

func main() {
    tracer := otel.Tracer("example-tracer")

    ctx, span := tracer.Start(context.Background(),
    "example-span")
    defer span.End()

    fmt.Println("Tracing example started")
}
```

With tracing, you can follow the flow of requests through your services and detect bottlenecks or failures across the entire system.

5. Best Practices for Error Handling and Debugging in Production

To ensure your Go applications are robust and manageable in production, follow these best practices:

- **Log Early and Log Often**: Logging should be used to capture important events, errors, and system state. Use structured logging for consistency and to make logs easier to search and analyze.
- **Use Context for Timeout and Cancellation**: Use the context package to manage request timeouts and cancellations, especially when dealing

with external services or long-running operations.

- **Graceful Shutdowns**: Use Go's context package and os.Signal to gracefully shut down applications and clean up resources.
- **Monitor Everything**: Use tools like Prometheus and Grafana for real-time metrics and alerts to monitor system health and performance.
- **Instrument Code with Traces**: Use OpenTelemetry to instrument your application with traces, allowing you to track performance issues and errors across distributed services.
- **Handle Panics Gracefully**: Always recover from panics in production systems to prevent application crashes, especially in long-running services like web servers.

In this chapter, we explored how to handle errors in Go, including custom error types, error wrapping, and best practices for error handling in production. We also discussed debugging techniques, using logs, pprof for profiling, and observability tools like Prometheus and OpenTelemetry. By applying these techniques, you can build resilient Go applications that handle errors gracefully, provide clear diagnostic information, and are easy to debug and monitor in production environments.

In the next chapter, we'll explore **testing strategies and writing robust unit tests** for Go applications, ensuring that your code is reliable and well-tested before it hits production.

The Future of Go: Trends and Latest Developments

As Go continues to evolve, its simplicity, efficiency, and strong concurrency model keep it a favorite among developers building scalable, reliable applications. Since its inception, Go has rapidly grown in popularity, thanks to its use in cloud computing, microservices, DevOps tooling, and backend web development. In this chapter, we will explore the latest trends and upcoming developments in the Go ecosystem, shedding light on how the language and its community are adapting to modern programming needs.

We'll cover:

- Upcoming Go language features and changes
- Trends in Go usage across industries
- Go's role in cloud-native and microservices architecture
- The Go ecosystem: Tooling, libraries, and frameworks
- The rise of generics and its impact on Go development
- Go's future in security, observability, and performance optimization

1. Upcoming Go Language Features and Changes

The Go team continually works on improving the language, focusing on stability, simplicity, and performance. As of the most recent releases, some exciting features and improvements are shaping the future of Go.

1.1 Go Generics (Released in Go 1.18)

The introduction of **generics** in Go 1.18 marked a significant evolution of the language. Generics enable developers to write more flexible and reusable code by allowing functions and types to operate on different data types without sacrificing type safety.

For example, with generics, you can write a function like this:

```
func Max[T any](a, b T) T {
    if a > b {
        return a
    }
    return b
}
```

This Max function can now accept arguments of any type that implements the comparison operator (>) without needing to write separate functions for each type (e.g., int, float64, string).

Generics will continue to evolve as the community adopts the feature more widely. Future updates may enhance the expressiveness of generics while maintaining Go's core simplicity.

1.2 Go 2: What to Expect

The Go team has hinted at long-term plans for a major update, tentatively referred to as **Go 2**. While details about Go 2 remain speculative, we can expect future developments to focus on:

- Improved error handling mechanisms
- Further simplifications to Go's concurrency model
- Enhancements to the standard library for better performance and scalability
- Continued focus on security and usability in cloud-native environments

While Go 2 is still on the horizon, Go 1.x will continue to see regular updates, with Go 1.20 and later versions introducing more incremental features.

2. Trends in Go Usage Across Industries

Go's strong performance and simplicity have led to its adoption across a wide range of industries. Several key sectors are driving the continued growth and popularity of Go:

2.1 Cloud-Native Development

Go has become the go-to language for cloud-native applications. With cloud providers like AWS, Google Cloud, and Microsoft Azure supporting Go as a first-class language, its role in **cloud infrastructure**, **serverless computing**, and **Kubernetes** ecosystems has solidified.

- **Kubernetes**: Written in Go, Kubernetes has accelerated Go's adoption in cloud-native environments. Developers working on Kubernetes-based platforms often use Go to extend functionality with custom controllers and operators.
- **DevOps Tooling**: Tools like **Terraform** (infrastructure as code), **Docker**, and **Prometheus** (monitoring) are built in Go, reinforcing its place in cloud and DevOps tooling.

2.2 Microservices and Distributed Systems

Go's lightweight concurrency model, efficient memory management, and ease of deployment make it ideal for building microservices and distributed systems. Companies like Netflix, Uber, and Dropbox use Go to power critical components of their microservices architectures.

- **Concurrency**: Go's goroutines allow developers to build highly concurrent microservices that can scale across distributed systems without the overhead of more complex thread management.
- **gRPC and Protobuf**: Go's built-in support for gRPC and Protocol Buffers makes it a strong choice for high-performance, low-latency service-to-service communication in microservices environments.

2.3 FinTech and Blockchain

Go is increasingly used in the **FinTech** and **blockchain** industries for building reliable, scalable backend services. Its strong type safety, fast compilation, and concurrency model are particularly suited to high-performance, real-time financial applications.

Projects like **Ethereum's go-ethereum (Geth)** client and various blockchain platforms use Go for building decentralized, distributed applications (dApps) and managing digital assets.

3. Go's Role in Cloud-Native and Microservices Architecture

As companies continue to embrace cloud-native architectures, Go's role in building scalable, resilient applications is becoming more prominent. With Go's lightweight runtime and focus on simplicity, it remains a top choice for building cloud-native microservices.

3.1 Go in Kubernetes and Container Orchestration

Kubernetes, one of the most widely used container orchestration platforms, is written in Go. The strong integration between Go and Kubernetes extends beyond just the core platform:

- **Custom Controllers and Operators**: Developers can use Go to write Kubernetes controllers and operators to automate complex workflows and manage application life cycles in Kubernetes clusters.
- **Helm**: Helm, the Kubernetes package manager, is another popular tool written in Go, making it easier for Go developers to manage Kubernetes applications.

3.2 Serverless Architectures

Go is well-suited for building **serverless applications**, where code is executed in response to events without managing servers. Popular serverless platforms like **AWS Lambda, Google Cloud Functions**, and **Azure Functions** support Go as a runtime, allowing developers to build lightweight serverless functions that execute quickly and efficiently.

3.3 Service Mesh with Go

Service mesh solutions, like **Istio** and **Linkerd**, are critical in managing the communication between microservices in a cloud-native architecture. These tools, often written in Go, help manage network traffic, security, and observability across distributed services.

4. The Go Ecosystem: Tooling, Libraries, and Frameworks

Go's ecosystem is growing rapidly, with a wide range of libraries, frameworks, and tools designed to help developers build applications faster and more efficiently. Some notable trends in the Go ecosystem include:

4.1 Web Frameworks and API Development

While Go's net/http package is sufficient for building web servers, a number of frameworks have emerged to simplify API development and web application design:

- **Gin**: One of the most popular web frameworks in Go, offering a lightweight, fast HTTP router with easy middleware support.
- **Echo**: Another fast, minimal web framework that supports RESTful APIs, WebSockets, and middleware.
- **Fiber**: A modern web framework inspired by Express.js, built on top of Go's fasthttp package for maximum performance.

4.2 Go Modules and Dependency Management

With the introduction of **Go Modules** in Go 1.11, Go's dependency management became more robust and efficient. Go modules allow developers to manage dependencies, handle versioning, and isolate project environments easily.

Key features of Go modules include:

- **Versioning**: Modules use semantic versioning to handle dependency versions, making it easy to manage and update dependencies.
- **No GOPATH Dependency**: Go modules remove the need for GOPATH, making it easier to structure projects and manage dependencies across multiple projects.

4.3 Popular Libraries for Go Development

Some of the most widely used libraries and tools in the Go ecosystem include:

- **gRPC**: For building high-performance, scalable microservices.
- **Cobra**: A widely used library for building CLI applications in Go.
- **Viper**: A configuration management library that supports environment variables, JSON, YAML, and more.
- **GORM**: An ORM (Object-Relational Mapping) library for interacting with SQL databases.

5. The Rise of Generics and Its Impact on Go Development

Generics were introduced in Go 1.18 and have opened new possibilities for Go developers, especially when it comes to writing reusable libraries and simplifying code that previously required type assertions or reflection.

5.1 Writing Generic Functions

Before generics, Go developers had to write separate functions for each type or use interfaces and reflection, which could lead to performance issues. With generics, developers can now write type-safe code without repetition.

For example, a generic Map function can be written like this:

```
func Map[T any](arr []T, f func(T) T) []T {
    result := make([]T, len(arr))
    for i, v := range arr {
        result[i] = f(v)
    }
    return result
}
```

This function works with any slice type and applies the transformation function f to each element.

5.2 Impact of Generics on Libraries and Frameworks

Generics will have a profound impact on libraries and frameworks in Go, allowing developers to build more powerful abstractions without compromising performance or type safety. For example, database libraries, like GORM, can now use generics to reduce boilerplate code and improve usability.

As the Go community continues to adopt generics, we can expect new design patterns and best practices to emerge, making Go more flexible while maintaining its hallmark simplicity.

6. Go's Future in Security, Observability, and Performance Optimization

As software systems grow more complex, the demand for tools and frameworks that improve security, observability, and performance will continue to increase. Go is well-positioned to meet these needs with its strong ecosystem of tools and libraries.

6.1 Security in Go Applications

Security is a top concern for developers, and Go's growing ecosystem of security tools is helping developers build more secure applications. Tools like **gosec** analyze Go code for security vulnerabilities, while libraries like **oauth2** and **jwt-go** make it easy to implement authentication and authorization in Go applications.

6.2 Observability: Monitoring, Tracing, and Logging

Go's support for **Prometheus, OpenTelemetry**, and structured logging tools like **Logrus** and **Zap** is driving improvements in observability. Developers can easily instrument their Go applications to track performance metrics, distributed traces, and logs, enabling them to identify and resolve issues in production systems.

6.3 Performance Optimization

Go's commitment to performance continues to evolve, with improvements in garbage collection, memory management, and CPU profiling. Tools like **pprof, Prometheus**, and **gopprof** make it easy for developers to profile and optimize their applications for maximum performance.

The future of Go looks bright, with a strong focus on simplicity, performance, and scalability. From the introduction of generics to Go's dominance in cloud-native development, the language continues to evolve to meet the needs of modern developers. As the Go ecosystem expands and new tools and libraries emerge, Go is poised to remain a top choice for building fast, reliable, and maintainable software systems.

In this chapter, we explored the latest developments and future trends in Go, including the impact of generics, Go's role in cloud-native and microservices architectures, and the future of security, observability, and performance optimization in Go applications. Go's growth in cloud computing, microservices, FinTech, and blockchain industries further cements its place as a modern programming language of choice for developers worldwide.